IMAGES
of America

SALT LAKE CITY'S
MODERN ARCHITECTURE

AERIAL VIEW OF SALT LAKE CITY. This pre-1960 aerial view of the downtown core shows the first beginnings of the modern city with the First Security Bank Building at the lower left-hand corner of the image. Modernism was integrated into the larger city but also replaced and redefined the city. (Courtesy Utah State Historical Society.)

IMAGES
of America

SALT LAKE CITY'S
MODERN ARCHITECTURE

Steven D. Cornell
and John D. Ewanowski

ARCADIA
PUBLISHING

Published by Arcadia Publishing
Charleston, South Carolina

Printed in the United States of America

Library of Congress Control Number: 2023937790

For all general information, please contact Arcadia Publishing:
Telephone 843-853-2070
Fax 843-853-0044
E-mail sales@arcadiapublishing.com

Visit us on the Internet at www.arcadiapublishing.com

To the visionaries, the architects, and the builders
who created the modern Salt Lake City

CONTENTS

ACKNOWLEDGMENTS

We are deeply grateful for the individuals who helped make this book a reality. We became acquainted while working at the architecture firm of CRSA in Salt Lake City and were both privileged to work with Allen Roberts and Wally Cooper, two pioneers in the Utah architectural preservation world. They are considered mentors and friends. We are equally grateful for the small preservation community in Salt Lake City who have supported our efforts in creating this book, especially Bim Oliver and Kirk Huffaker, both of whom have narrated the stories of Modernism in their own eloquent and insightful style. We consulted the Utah Center for Architecture's Utah Architects Project database to cross-reference designers and dates. We are grateful to the staff at the Utah State Historical Society (USHS) for their tireless help in providing the bulk of the images for this work. We began this book pre-Covid, and then as soon as that started, the Salt Lake City area suffered a moderate earthquake in March 2020, damaging the collections repository in the historic Rio Grande Depot. Over the course of nearly three years, the team there boxed up and moved the entire collection to temporary facilities in anticipation of the restoration of that fine building. Finally opening their new space in early 2023, Doug Misner and Greg Walz were our fearless leaders and provided the bulk of the images in very short order. We thank the efforts of the staff at the University of Utah Special Collections (UUSC) and the staff of Westminster University's Giovale Library (WUGL). We acknowledge the patience of the Arcadia team during this long process and give special thanks to Caitrin Cunningham, our editor. We began this journey in 2017 with our Uncommon Modern Salt Lake project, which was a collective effort to inventory the remaining modern buildings in Salt Lake County. There were many individuals involved in this endeavor, and we hope to give thanks to you all here. A few we wish to name include Joseph Milillo, Kenneth Wheadon, Roger Roper, Cody Derrick, Benji Pearson, Jonathon Love, Darlene Fuhst, and Brennan Schultz. Finally, we wish to thank our local statewide nonprofit preservation organization, Preservation Utah; its board of trustees; its former executive director, David Amott; and its current executive director, Brandy Strand, who have enabled us over the years to do what we love.

INTRODUCTION

When the Mormon pioneers arrived in the Salt Lake Valley on July 24, 1847, led by an ailing Brigham Young, they immediately began the process of urbanization, laying out the Temple Block first, known as "Temple Square," and then an additional 134 blocks in a 9 by 15 grid. The Salt Lake plat was based on the "plat of Zion"—a utopian city planning concept developed by Joseph Smith, the young faith's founder, in Kirtland, Ohio, in the early 1830s—and was comprised of large 660-foot-square blocks with the sacred church-owned public buildings at its center. The church had attempted to lay down such city grids in various locations throughout the western frontier of the United States (present-day Utah was Mexican territory at the time), but they were persecuted and run out of Kirtland, Ohio; Far West, Missouri; and Nauvoo, Illinois. The land in Utah was sparsely populated by the Shoshone, Ute, Paiute, and Goshute tribes, but the Church of Jesus Christ of Latter-day Saints (LDS) found a location in Salt Lake City where they could build their millennial Zion and end their long migration. The city's gridded streets were numbered based on their proximity to Temple Square and their cardinal direction.

Following the Treaty of Guadalupe Hidalgo, which ended the Mexican-American War, the Mexican lands became a part of the United States and were incorporated into the new Utah Territory, with the City of the Great Salt Lake formally established. With Young as its first governor, the theocratic Utah Territory provided fertile ground for the LDS Church to grow. The Mormon migration to the Salt Lake Valley continued for decades, and thus, most of the first non-native inhabitants of the Salt Lake Valley were Mormon pioneers.

Salt Lake City's first boom coincided with the growth of the LDS Church and businesses to support this growth, along with other industries tied into the economies of the American West. The Utah Central Railroad was built to the city from the main transcontinental line at Ogden. Fort Douglas was established during the Civil War as an outpost of the US Army. Mining companies that had started in Park City or Bingham Canyon built headquarters downtown, along with palatial mansions for their founders. Luxury hotels were built to house visiting dignitaries and businessmen, while resorts sprang up around the Great Salt Lake.

By the time Utah gained statehood in 1896, with Salt Lake City as its capital, the city's population had reached about 50,000 inhabitants. The south end of the city reached 900 South Street (nine blocks south of Temple Square), with vast open agricultural lands beyond. The population continued to climb through World War I and the Great Depression. The Beaux-Arts–style Utah State Capitol was completed in 1916 and was clad in the same granite as the Salt Lake Temple. A public airstrip was built on the west side of the city, initially for mail delivery and then for passenger travel. With the University of Utah occupying its present location on the benches of Salt Lake's east side, after Congress deeded the university 60 acres of land at Fort Douglas, it began to bloom in its current location around President's Circle. Professional baseball came to town in 1911 with the Union Association's Salt Lake Skyscrapers, and after the league folded, the Salt Lake Bees of the Pacific Coast League were formed.

In 1940, the final census before World War II broke out, 150,000 people lived in Salt Lake City proper, an exponential increase since the time of the pioneers. The process of urbanization was put on hold for a few years as Salt Lakers focused on the war effort, both serving in the armed forces and supporting them from home.

This book focuses on what happened to Salt Lake City beginning at that time, as the United States was slowly surfacing from the Great Depression and when soldiers began coming home to start their families. The GI Bill led to exploding numbers of students in higher education, and after a generation that had witnessed the Great Depression and World War II, they now finally had leisure time and money to spend on recreational activities. With the rapid population growth, the construction of new civic buildings, churches, schools, stores, and offices was on the rise.

Modernist architecture had started to trickle into the Utah vernacular by the time World War II put a hold on large-scale building projects. The Prairie style, Art Deco, and Streamline Moderne were integrated into downtown offices and church buildings along the urbanized Wasatch Front but especially in downtown Salt Lake City. The Utah Chapter of the American Institute of Architects released a futuristic plan for the Utah State Fairpark in the middle of the war as a way to engage out-of-work architects. Skyscrapers in Salt Lake City—as early as the Walker Bank Building (1911)—used steel structures to reach greater heights and higher density. The LDS Church as well had been using proto-Modernist approaches on its ward chapels and temples in the early 20th century.

If one individual could be seen as the progenitor of Utah Modernism, it would be Roger Bailey, the first chair of the University of Utah's Department of Architecture. Bailey was a professor of architecture at the University of Michigan when he stopped over for a one-night stay in Salt Lake City during the summer of 1948 with his wife on the way to the West Coast. Legend has it (as recorded from an oral history by Peter Goss) that Bailey got 15 miles outside of Salt Lake City the next morning when he realized that three of his Michigan students were from Utah. Wondering why these three would go so far afield for their architectural education before returning home to practice, Bailey turned the car around to pay a visit to University of Utah president A. Ray Olpin, who gave him one day to prepare an outline of what would be required to start a bona fide architecture school at the university. Bailey used the opportunity to record his thoughts on architectural education of the time and would write Olpin a letter outlining how they could be applied in Salt Lake.

Meanwhile, the University of Utah had absorbed 340 acres of new campus land that had been a part of Fort Douglas. In need of immediate guidance, Olpin called Bailey in Ann Arbor, before he could get the letter off, to inquire about his availability to help plan the new campus and teach architecture at the expanding school. Bailey was surprised when he arrived in 1949 to learn that the architectural instruction would begin immediately, along with the campus planning Olpin thought Bailey would be prioritizing. With urgency, Bailey set up space in an abandoned basement on campus and started teaching 45 students straightaway.

Enrollment at the University of Utah had increased from 400 before the end of the war to 10,000 in the five years following, and Roger Bailey was the right man to guide the architecture program into the new era. Having completed his studies at Cornell University and the Ecole des Beaux-Arts in Paris, Bailey was a student of classicism and history, but he was also a forward-thinking designer, as evidenced by his 1930 prize-winning design for a Chicago war memorial along with Eric Gugler. Although it was never realized, the design featured a 200-foot-tall unadorned cenotaph. Bailey hired an impressive faculty at the University of Utah, including Jim Ackland from Syracuse University, Gordon Heck and Donald Panushka from Massachusetts Institute of Technology (MIT), and Charles Moore from the University of Michigan, who would go on to be a prominent Postmodernist architect with projects like Sea Ranch in California.

Bailey hired a few more faculty members from MIT, which was then (as now) at the cutting edge of architectural design education, and soon the Modernist influence was tangible in the design portfolios of University of Utah architecture graduates. Most of these graduates were in-state and remained in Utah following graduation, thus forming the core of Salt Lake's architecture profession as the building boom found its footing in the early 1960s. Robert Bliss—also a product of MIT—succeeded Bailey as the head of the Department of Architecture in 1963. Those young architects of the Bailey era would go on to fuel their own local avant-garde, both as principals of their own emerging firms and as young designers injecting a Modernist sensibility into already established firms.

The Modernism of the University of Utah Department of Architecture found an unlikely ally in David Oman McKay, who became the ninth president of the LDS Church in 1951 and oversaw a sweeping building boom locally, nationally, and internationally. During McKay's tenure, the LDS Church built temples in Switzerland, Los Angeles, New Zealand, London, and Oakland, all of which were constructed in a Modernist vernacular style. Countless ward chapels were built in the Salt Lake Valley to bring church services to new suburban developments, and these generally espoused Modernist design to reflect the corresponding modernization of the church itself. Perhaps the most future-thinking architectural achievement of McKay's presidency was the Mormon Pavilion at the 1964 World's Fair in Queens, which incorporated a vertically enhanced re-creation of the Salt Lake Temple's east facade flanked with modernist wings, fusing a traditional LDS architectural style with the futurism of the Space Age.

Back in Salt Lake City, the Utah Chapter of the American Institute of Architects, evoking their futuristic 1945 master plan for the Utah State Fairpark, began organizing the Second Century Plan to envision what the next 100 years of civic development might look like. The Downtown Development Association Inc. was the organization that formally authored the Second Century Plan in 1962, and it included a development committee of American Institute of Architects (AIA) members. Architect Dean Gustavson served as the chair of the committee and was joined by a who's who of the emerging architectural avant-garde, including Donald Panushka (vice chairman), Richard Stringham (secretary), Martin Brixen, John Sugden, William Rowe Smith, George Cannon Young, and R. Lloyd Snedaker.

Three years after their vision for downtown Salt Lake City was published, the Downtown Development Association followed it up with a 1965 progress report and listed the following projects as realizations of the plan: the convention center, the Social Hall Avenue development, the main parking mall, Wolfe's parking ramp, the Paris parking area, the library (the conversion of the old library into the Hansen Planetarium), the Main Street mall project, the State Street tree planting, the LDS parking and administrative building, the Zion's Co-operative Mercantile Institute (ZCMI) mall development, organization of the Downtown Planning Association, and the enactment of urban renewal law. While critics saw the Second Century Plan as a Robert Moses–style, heavy-handed urban renewal, it was clear that the plan was being implemented and was leaving a lasting impression on downtown.

By the end of the 1960s, downtown Salt Lake City had transformed itself with numerous skyscrapers, civic buildings, and housing projects. After the construction of the International-style First Security Bank Building, a product of Los Angeles designer W.A. Sarmiento with local architect Slack Winburn, most of these new Modernist landmarks became the work of local architects. The Modernist projects proliferated outward from downtown to the University of Utah and Westminster College campuses, to Sugar House and the West side, and to Capitol Hill and the Avenues neighborhood. In other words, Modernism became an indelible part of the city fabric that remains intact to this day.

In the 50 years since Modernism reached its peak in Salt Lake City and Utah more broadly, the ebbs and flows of architectural periods were felt, especially with Postmodernism as the abrupt blowback to Modernism, then Neoclassicism as our institutions morphed around the fervor of national conservatism and traditionalism of the bicentennial zeitgeist, eventually leading to Deconstructivism. Modernism was influential in these evolutionary trends but inhabited a cultural moment conveyed in concrete, steel, and glass; straight lines; and purely formal designs.

This book is meant to evoke that architectural moment locally in Salt Lake City—not as a comprehensive catalog of its features, but by marking its high points, its common points, and in some cases its low points, when a progressive group of architects, urban planners, community leaders, enterprising business people, and citizens saw the future and built it.

One

CIVIC AND PUBLIC
ARCHITECTURE

SECOND CENTURY PLAN,
1962. Architect Dean
Gustavson, pictured here,
served as chair of the
Development Committee of
the Downtown Development
Association Inc., which
published the Second
Century Plan in 1962. In
the photograph, Gustavson
points to the planned
Church Office Building,
one of the visionary projects
of the Second Century
Plan, while the convention/
cultural center (realized as
the Salt Palace) model is
visible in the foreground
with a rendering mounted
behind him. The plan
identified 10 projects—some
of which were already under
construction—to spark a
downtown revival considered
necessary by its authors,
including developers,
urban planners, business
owners, and politicians.
(Courtesy USHS.)

FEDERAL RESERVE BANK, 1959. The Federal Reserve Bank of San Francisco opened this Salt Lake City branch in 1959. It was the fourth building to house the Salt Lake branch, which first opened in 1918. The previous structure was on the southwest corner of South Temple and State Streets. The building was designed by Ashton, Evans & Brazier Architects and constructed by Tolboe and Harlin Construction Company at a cost of $3 million. The reinforced concrete and steel structure was faced with polished granite and a ceramic veneer. The unassuming, austere structure rises three stories above State Street with three underground floors, the lowest housing a huge vault for currency storage. (Courtesy USHS.)

STATE OFFICE BUILDING, 1961. Scott and Beecher designed the State Office Building, situated immediately north of the state capitol, which broke ground on March 9, 1959, to fanfare. Sen. Haven J. Barolo (R-Layton) sponsored the bill to build the $3-million complex, which was constructed by the Alfred Brown Company. Despite its modern form, the structure was clad in cast stone meant to resemble— and harmonize with—the Richard Kletting–designed capitol (1916). The complex included a distinct circular glass cafeteria for government employees. The State Office Building was unveiled on June 9, 1961, in a ceremony led by Gov. George D. Clyde. It was demolished in 2022 to make way for a new $165-million North Capitol Building after the modern structure was deemed spatially and seismically insufficient and after the state moved a majority of its offices to an existing building in Taylorsville. (Above, courtesy UUSC; right, courtesy USHS.)

WOODWARD FIELD, 1920. Salt Lake City opened Woodward Field in 1920 to handle mail movements across the West. Commercial flights began in 1926 when Ben Redman and J.A. Tomlinson rode in a mail plane to Los Angeles in the inaugural flight of Western Airlines. Charles Lindbergh visited Woodward Field in the *Spirit of St. Louis* in 1927. The field was renamed Salt Lake City Municipal Airport in 1930. As air travel became more common for Salt Lakers, the need for a modern passenger terminal was recognized, and a $2.5-million bond issue was approved on January 13, 1959. City Commissioner L.C. Romney was instrumental in gaining public approval for the new terminal and in securing funding through the bond issue and other city, state, and federal funding streams. The aerial image below is a view of the new buildings in 1961. (Both, courtesy USHS.)

SALT LAKE CITY MUNICIPAL AIRPORT, 1961.
The Jet Age structure cost $4.5 million by
the time it was completed for a June 17, 1961,
dedication ceremony attended by LDS Church
president David O. McKay, Mayor J. Bracken
Lee, and Gov. George D. Clyde. Five airlines
operated out of the new terminal: Frontier,
Bonanza, United, Western, and West Coast.
Phoenix, Jackson Hole, Albuquerque, and
Cedar City were some of the popular early
destinations. Ashton, Evans & Brazier served
as the architects of the terminal building.
One distinct feature of the terminal was a
world map set in terrazzo that was built by the
J. Bartoli Company of Dallas, Texas, which
countless passengers walked across over the
six decades the terminal was in service. The
airport became very popular, especially as a
major Delta hub, while expanding into new
concourses to the west. A new airport terminal
(Phase I) was completed in 2020 to handle
the tens of millions of passengers flowing
through what is now the Salt Lake International
Airport every year, and the historic terminal—
along with its crowd-pleasing terrazzo world
map—was razed. (Both, courtesy USHS.)

METROPOLITAN COMPLEX, 1961–1968. On September 12, 1961, Salt Lake City voters went to the polls to vote on a $19.5-million bond that included a new central library and the Metropolitan Hall of Justice, which housed the city police, county sheriff, and jail. Harold K. Beecher, a graduate of the University of Michigan School of Architecture and designer of the Salt Palace, convention center, numerous buildings for Brigham Young University, and Salt Lake City's Federal Building, served as the master architect for the complex. (Courtesy USHS.)

MAIN LIBRARY, 1964. When the old Salt Lake City Library on State Street was converted to the Hansen Planetarium in the early 1960s, the library moved to the Metropolitan Complex with a dedication ceremony on October 30, 1964, about a week after the building's champion and library board chairman Gail Plummer passed away. The primary material of the library exterior is Mo-Cai, exposed aggregate precast concrete, a relatively rare local building material at the time. The *Deseret News* touted, "The ultra-modern structure, one of few boasting escalators, resembles a modern art museum more than the old concept of libraries." The New Formalist library was designed by Edwards & Daniels Architects. In 2003, the city library moved to a new building designed by Safdie Architects on the site of the Metropolitan Hall of Justice, and the 1964 library now houses The Leonardo museum. (Both, courtesy USHS.)

METROPOLITAN HALL OF JUSTICE, 1966. The Metropolitan Hall of Justice was a 50-50 investment by Salt Lake City and Salt Lake County, although the negotiation between the two was slightly fraught, especially given the turf war between the city police and county sheriff. Construction inspections revealed cases of shoddy concrete and wiring, and architect Harold Beecher had to defend some design shortcomings, which he claimed were dictated by the city, county, and advisory board. The jail finally opened in July 1966 after delays. The building was demolished in 2001 to make way for the new main library. (Courtesy USHS.)

COURTS BUILDING, 1968. The final structure built as a part of the Metropolitan Complex was the Salt Lake Courts Building, also designed by Harold Beecher. While the Metropolitan Hall of Justice was under construction, the need for additional courtrooms arose. The distinct mosaic concrete on the Salt Lake Courts Building set it apart from its Metropolitan Complex cousins, and a war memorial flagpole was built in the contemporaneously completed plaza, unifying all the buildings together. The Salt Lake Courts Building was also demolished in 2001 in anticipation of the redevelopment of the block for the new main library. (Courtesy USHS.)

TENTH EAST SENIOR CENTER, 1963. Burtch W. Beall Jr. and Paul Lemione served as the architects with George S. Nicolatus as planner for the "Elder Citizens' Center," which was constructed by the Culp Construction Company immediately in front of the existing senior center at 245 South Tenth East, and it opened with a special tour on July 11, 1963. The building features a distinctive patinated copper fascia, the pattern of which is carried over into concrete masonry units that provide its structure. It blends seamlessly into the neighborhood and surrounding landscape. The Tenth East Senior Center is still operated by Salt Lake County Aging and Adult Services. (Courtesy Steven Cornell.)

Bennett Federal Building, 1964. The Federal Building was completed in 1964 and named after US senator Wallace Bennett, who represented Utah from 1951 to 1975, in 1985. The eight-story building cost $10.5 million to construct and was designed by Deseret Architects and Engineers, along with Snedaker, Budd, Monroe & Associates. The design was lauded for its street-level plaza, an uncommon amenity in Utah at the time, which featured a fountain sculpture by Angelo Caravaglia. The building still stands but was heavily overhauled in 2001 to meet modern security standards and seismic requirements. (Courtesy USHS.)

Two

RELIGIOUS ARCHITECTURE

GRANDVIEW WARD, 1938. Construction of the new Grandview Ward chapel at 2940 East 2000 South was begun in September 1937, and the building was dedicated in July 1938 by Heber J. Grant, then president of the LDS Church. The ward chapel and adjoining amusement hall were completed after 10 months' work at a cost of $55,000. As reported in the July 10, 1938, *Salt Lake Tribune*, the structure was "modern in architecture" and contained "many unique features," including an off-center speaker's stand and domed skylight. Glass brick and reinforced concrete were used in the construction of the building. Lowell E. Parrish was the architect who worked alongside Arthur Price, general supervisor of the church's building program. (Courtesy USHS.)

BRYAN WARD, 1939. Groundbreaking for the new chapel at 1621 South 1100 East took place in April 1939. J. Reuben Clark, then first counselor in the LDS Church's First Presidency, dedicated the new Bryan Ward in November 1941. The boxy brick building, which was completed at a cost of $55,000, was designed by Edwin O. Anderson and built by Howard L. McKean. (Courtesy USHS.)

TWELFTH WARD CHAPEL, 1941. Plans for the chapel were drawn up by architect A.B. Paulson at the outset of World War II and were of a "modernized Georgian" design, according to the June 16, 1939, *Salt Lake Telegram*. The building was to have "a red brick facing, a slate roof over the towered portions, and a positive ventilating system," reported the June 20, 1939, *Deseret News*. The presiding bishopric of the LDS Church approved an appropriation of $42,000 for the construction of the chapel in August 1939, and ground was broken on September 26, 1939, for the new chapel at 630 East 100 South. As part of the effort to fund the new chapel, a bake sale was held with "home-made cakes and pies" sold by members of the Relief Society. The funds on hand were exhausted by February 1940, and construction was halted until September, when enough funds had been secured to complete the building in the spring of 1941. (Courtesy USHS.)

IVINS WARD, 1943. The Ivins Ward chapel construction was initiated in early 1940 at a banquet for the benefit of the building fund with 400 persons attending. The groundbreaking would not happen until September 1941, however, at which there were 200 people in attendance, including Antoine R. Ivins, son of the late Anthony W. Ivins, for whom the ward was named. Lowell E. Parrish was the architect of the chapel, located at 300 East Garfield Avenue. The Ivins Ward was dedicated in December 1943 with David O. McKay, second counselor in the First Presidency, presiding. (Courtesy USHS.)

LDS INSTITUTE BUILDING, 1950. Begun in 1947, the $325,000 building for the Institute of Religion at the University of Utah at 274 South University Street was described as both practical and beautiful. Pope and Thomas Architects designed the 35,000-square-foot building, and McKean Construction built it. The chapel could accommodate 435 persons; however, when it was dedicated by George Albert Smith, LDS Church president, on January 1, 1950, a total of 3,000 people crowded into the chapel for the occasion. (Courtesy USHS.)

PARLEY'S CANYON WARD, 1953. The Parley's Canyon Ward had been meeting in a little red schoolhouse for 63 years when, following two years of construction, the Parley's Canyon Ward chapel at 2100 East Parley's Canyon Boulevard was dedicated in December 1953 by David O. McKay, president of the LDS Church. McKay commended the bishopric of the ward for the work done to complete the edifice and the ward membership for their spirit of gratitude and appreciation. (Courtesy USHS.)

ROSE PARK SOUTH BAPTIST CHURCH, 1955. The Rose Park South Baptist Church was still in its infancy in Salt Lake when it announced plans to erect a new building for worship on the southeast corner of 1100 West and 600 North. The L-shaped building would be constructed around their current prefabricated structure on the corner that had been in use since 1952. Groundbreaking ceremonies were held in July 1952. The entry to the sanctuary was placed at the intersection of the two wings, where there was also a "brick tower" extending about 50 feet into the air "surmounted by a copper finial," according to the July 24, 1954, *Salt Lake Tribune*. Anticipating a four-month construction period, the church still needed some "painting, floor finishing and acoustic tile" before the planned first services on Palm Sunday in April 1955, as reported in the April 2, 1955, *Salt Lake Tribune*. (Courtesy USHS.)

HOLY TRINITY LUTHERAN, 1955. The Holy Trinity Mission was launched in 1952 in a residence in Rose Park, and by the fall of 1954, plans for a new edifice at 1142 West 900 North were unveiled by Haines and Purhonen Architects. The first unit included a nave, sacristy, chancel, classrooms, office, and kitchen but would eventually become the parish hall once the main church, tower, Sunday school, and parsonage were constructed. The interior was to feature A-frame trusses with seven of the nine having large crosses near the ceiling. The new building was estimated to cost $20,000. Construction on the small church began in November 1954 and was completed in May 1955. (Courtesy USHS.)

ENSIGN WARD, 1955. The Ensign Ward chapel was designed as a "rambler-style, split-level meeting house" on Ninth Avenue and K Street, according to the June 18, 1955, *Salt Lake Tribune*. Groundbreaking occurred in March 1953, and by February 1954, though still incomplete, meetings were being held. The building was dedicated in June 1955 by then LDS president David O. McKay. One feature of the building was the Sky Room, which provided a "sweeping view of the entire Salt Lake Valley." (Courtesy USHS.)

Park Stake Center, 1955. The Park Stake Center was planned as a multipurpose facility, housing recreation and athletic programs and capable of seating between 500 and 1,000 persons. Groundbreaking ceremonies were conducted in June 1952 with a cornerstone placement ceremony in December of that same year. On hand at the cornerstone ceremony was Elder Mark E. Peterson of the Council of the Twelve Apostles. The president of the Stake, Charles B. Richmond, conducted the ceremony with architect Henry P. Fetzer and mason Thomas B. Child, who is known for his creation of Gilgal Gardens in Salt Lake City. Although the $300,000 building was being used by 1954, it was not dedicated until December 1955 by LDS Church president David O. McKay. (Courtesy USHS.)

CRYSTAL HEIGHTS, 1956. Members of the Crystal Heights Ward got the first glimpse of their new chapel at a banquet in November 1952. The new chapel was designed by architects Emil and John Fetzer (Fetzer and Fetzer Architects), and the building incorporated many unusual features, including "the modern trend of bringing the outside into the inside through use of large picture windows," as reported in the November 22, 1952, *Salt Lake Tribune*. The groundbreaking was in May 1953. Located at 2000 East and Stratford Avenue, the chapel was dedicated in September 1956 by Elder Richard L. Evans of the Council of the Twelve Apostles. (Courtesy USHS.)

ZION EVANGELICAL LUTHERAN CHURCH, 1956. With plans for the new $200,000 Zion Evangelical Lutheran Church on 2100 East and Foothill Boulevard nearing completion by the end of 1954, groundbreaking ceremonies were planned for December of that same year. Designed by the architectural firm of Ashton, Evans & Brazier, the building was deemed "Ultra Modern" with steeply arcing rooflines and a 90-foot belfry. The church would house a 14-room educational unit, a fellowship hall, a choir room, and a nave capable of seating 300 persons, with moving partitions at the rear to add an additional 100 seats. The organ from the old church (pictured below) was rebuilt and reinstalled in the new edifice. The belfry would house the original bells from the former church (1891), a Gothic Revival building downtown on the northwest corner 200 South and 400 East. By the 1950s, the downtown location was too far from where the population centers were trending in the southeastern part of the city. Worship services were held for the first time in the new building in October 1956. (Both, courtesy USHS.)

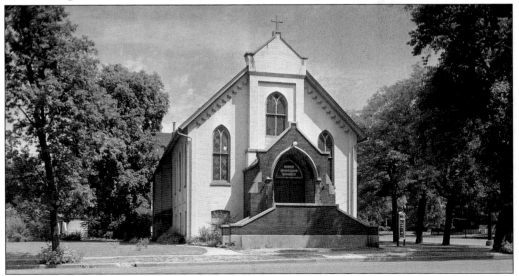

SALT LAKE BUDDHIST CHURCH, 1962. The Salt Lake Buddhist Church was organized in 1912 and was originally located on South Temple Street before moving in 1924 to a new building on 100 South in what was known as Japantown. Plans were announced in 1961 for the new structure, which was to be located on the corner of 100 South and 100 West. The architect was Taka Kida, a member of the Buddhist congregation and an architect representing Paul K. Evans Architects of Salt Lake City. The $120,000 building was modern but adorned with traditional Japanese details. The building would house a chapel with a seating capacity of 160, a recreation hall, a patio garden, classrooms, offices, and a kitchen and would serve the area's 600 local Buddhists. (Both, courtesy USHS.)

St. Joseph's Villa, 1959. St. Joseph's Villa was a home for the aged located at 1910 South 500 East and was run by the Sisters of Charity of the Incarnate Word of Galveston, Texas. The new and modern St. Joseph's Villa replaced the 1892 landmark Victorian residence, which was demolished, and could house 70 persons, a substantial increase. The architects were Albert S. Golemon of Houston, Texas, and B.E. Brazier (Ashton, Evans & Brazier) of Salt Lake City. (Courtesy Steven Cornell.)

University Stake Complex, 1964–1965. The $1.4-million University Stake Complex adjacent to the University of Utah was conceived to fill a growing need at the university and provide students "spiritual guidance and Church leadership," reported the December 5, 1964, *Deseret News*. Designed by architect John N. Clawson, the complex included three chapels—each with gymnasiums, classrooms, and cultural halls—on a 32-acre parcel at the corner of Hempstead Road and Foothill Boulevard. The large complex, erected by Fredrickson Construction, also included a new institute facility, which would complement the one already built on University Street. (Courtesy Steven Cornell.)

MOUNT TABOR LUTHERAN CHURCH, 1909. The small congregation had occupied the structure at First Avenue and E Street in Salt Lake's Avenues neighborhood for a half century and had ultimately outgrown the facility. Designed by Richard K.A. Kletting, dean of Utah architecture, the small Gothic Revival church adorning a corner of the Avenues was built for Tabor Lutheran Church, organized in 1907 by Danish immigrants. At the time, the congregation consisted of 33 adults. (Courtesy USHS.)

MOUNT TABOR LUTHERAN CHURCH, 1964. In 1960, Rev. Arthur Sorensen, pastor of the Tabor Lutheran Church, announced plans to move his congregation to a new building on 200 South and 700 East. The groundbreaking for the new church was held in January 1963 for what was called "one of Utah's most unusual church buildings" in the January 5, 1963, *Salt Lake Tribune.* The church was circular in design and was based on a "historic Scandinavian heritage echoing many of the churches of round design found in Denmark," according to Pastor Sorensen. (Courtesy USHS.)

MOUNT TABOR LUTHERAN CHURCH, INTERIOR. Dedicatory services for the newly designed church were planned for March 1964 with Dr. William Larsen, secretary of the American Lutheran Church of Minneapolis, presiding. The new church was designed as a "friendly church" and that is why "it is built in the round," explained Pastor Sorensen in the March 7, 1964, *Salt Lake Tribune.* The altar was positioned in the center as a focal point of worship. The design was executed by Charles D. Peterson of Panushka and Peterson Architects of Salt Lake City. The project was built by the John De Young Construction Company. (Courtesy USHS.)

FIRST CONGREGATIONAL CHURCH, 1893. The First Congregational Church was the oldest Protestant church in Salt Lake City. Organized in 1865, they built a Gothic Revival–style church at 402 East 100 South in 1893 that would be their home for 71 years until it was replaced with their new church in 1965 (next page). (Courtesy USHS.)

First Congregational Church, 1965. Groundbreaking ceremonies for the congregation's new $400,000 church at 2150 Foothill Drive were held in July 1964, and the first services were held Easter Sunday 1965. The church featured a "500-seat sanctuary, a kitchen, offices, recreation and social areas, restrooms, and a study," according to the September 18, 1965, *Deseret News*. It combined parts and pieces of the old structure (pictured on the previous page), including the "colorful stained glass windows and a beautiful pipe organ," as reported in the September 11, 1965, *Salt Lake Tribune*. One stained-glass window depicted the "Walk to Emmaus" after a painting by Bernhard Plockhorst and was built by J. and R. Lamb of New York. The pipe organ was built by Farrand and Votey and installed in the original sanctuary in 1893. When it was reinstalled in the new sanctuary, the organ was equipped with 2,475 pipes. The old church was purchased by the Salt Lake City Board of Education with the intent to demolish the building to make way for its new headquarters, but arsons got to it first, and it was destroyed in a fire in June 1965. The new church was designed by Edwards & Daniels Architects and built by the Cannon Construction Company. (Courtesy UUSC.)

LDS Bureau of Information, 1904. In late 1960, excavation was underway for a new Bureau of Information Building on Temple Square. The new building would replace the former Bureau of Information (pictured) and was necessary to accommodate the more than 150 volunteer guides and the thousands of visitors coming to Temple Square annually. Because it was located against the northwest corner of the site, steel pilings were driven to protect the pioneer-constructed stone walls. The excavation reached 25 feet deep, and Paulson Construction was hired to perform the work. (Courtesy USHS.)

LDS Bureau of Information, 1963–1966. By March 1963, the new structure was completed and the dedication scheduled; however, the building would serve initially as a temporary temple annex for two years until the permanent annex was completed. Once the structure was put into service as the Bureau of Information, the idea of a visitors center was just beginning to take shape, but as late as 1966, the building was still referred to using the former title. Rather than mounting exhibits for history buffs, the visitors center concept was meant to attract masses of people to a center filled with the latest audiovisual displays, beautiful paintings, and statues. Once the new annex was completed in 1966, the building was "unremodeled," returning it to its intended use, which included the installation of 13 mural paintings portraying the life of Jesus by Sydney E. King of Milford, Virginia. By 1967, a total of 1.25 million tourists were visiting annually. The role of the building eventually increased, becoming a hub in the already bustling downtown. Additional visitors centers were created in other locations patterned after the flagship Salt Lake City program. (Both, courtesy USHS.)

St. Ambrose Catholic Church, 1948, 1964. The Salt Lake parish of St. Ambrose Catholic Church was established in 1948 with the appointment of Fr. Joseph Gosselin as pastor, and plans were immediately implemented to construct a church on 2300 East between 1900 and 2000 South. The small parish continued to grow, and by 1963, a main sanctuary building was under construction. The contractor was Williams and Peterson Construction Company. The architects were Folsom and Hunt (R. Bruce Folsom and McCown E. Hunt). The new church would be the second-largest Catholic church in Utah and would feature a sanctuary with a three-ton, pressed-stone altar fully visible from all parts of the sanctuary. Sandblasted concrete columns supported the pre-stressed concrete beams of the roof, which allowed for unobstructed views. The walls were finished in pressed stone and birchwood and polished to a semigloss by Buehner Block of Salt Lake. A 14-foot-high crucifix carved of elm wood from Italy hung above the altar. The stained-glass windows, each 20 feet high and 13 feet wide, were made of mosaics of colored glass. The church, which seated 950, including the choir, was described in the December 12, 1964, *Salt Lake Tribune* as "modern in structure, contemporary in style and unique in that it 'fans out' from the 55-foot width at the altar to an 88-foot width at the back." The new building cost $600,000. It was dedicated in May 1965 with 1,000 persons participating. (Courtesy Steven Cornell.)

St. Ann's Catholic Church, 1968. The longstanding dream of the 500 congregants still meeting in a small parish church at St. Ann's Catholic School was soon to be realized in their new triangular-shaped church, which was under construction in 1967. The iconic design of the $415,000 St. Ann's Catholic Church at 430 East 2100 South focused all of its attention on the sanctuary and altar, with the roof sweeping skyward from the west entry to where a nine-foot linden-wood carved statue of the risen Christ, weighing 585 pounds, hovered above the altar. A series of narrow windows just below the roofline provided ethereal lighting of the interior space. Architect William "Will" Louie of Scott, Louie, and Browning Architects maximized the contrast between the modern church and the Victorian-style orphanage school to the west. Culp Construction Company built the church, which in form represented the bridge between heaven and earth by ascending from the ground to one high peak, according to Fr. Frank Brusatto. (Courtesy USHS.)

Three

COMMERCIAL AND OFFICE ARCHITECTURE

FIRST SECURITY BANK BUILDING, 1955. George Eccles (seated) is pictured with, from left to right, Slack Winburn, architect; Harry Moyer, architect; and William Cannon. Hailed in the January 7, 1954, *Salt Lake Tribune* as the "largest building program in downtown Salt Lake in approximately three decades," the First Security Bank Building is considered the best example of the International Style of architecture in Utah. At 12 stories, the contemporary and modern structure consisted of four distinct volumes: the main volume, a nine-story transparent office tower that resided atop a two-story horizontal base, a 10-story elevator and stair tower standing behind the main volume, and a three-story annex extending to the south. The distinctive volumes are further individualized with color, the utilitarian massings in a muted red and the functional office volumes in white. (Courtesy USHS.)

FIRST SECURITY BANK BUILDING, MATERIALS. Rising 191 feet, it rests on 236 concrete piles driven to refusal on the corner of 400 South and Main Street. Enclosing 105,000 square feet of space, it was said to contain an additional 5,000 square feet over a traditional masonry building due to its wafer-thin three-inch skin. Ribbon windows line each of the floors of the main volume and wrap around the three north, east, and west faces. The same windows on the east and west facades contained tinted glass, while the south-facing windows on the "back side" of the building were equipped with aluminum sunshades. The thin curtain wall skin consists of a combination of glass, steel, aluminum, and porcelain enameled metal panels, which were intended to protect the steel. (Courtesy USHS.)

FIRST SECURITY BANK BUILDING, DESIGNERS. Utah's largest safe deposit box was installed in the vault with 2,501 boxes. Topping off the tower, in 10-foot-tall block letters, were the words "First Security Bank" proudly announcing the building as the bank's new home. The building was designed by Peruvian American architect Wenceslao Alfonso "W.A." Sarmiento and W.G. Knoebel, both of the Bank Building Corporation of St. Louis, as well as Harry Moyer out of the San Francisco office and prominent Salt Lake City architect Slack W. Winburn acting as the local architect. The Utah Construction Company, a subsidiary of the First Security Corporation, was the general contractor. (Courtesy USHS.)

SURETY LIFE INSURANCE BUILDING, 1957. Surety Life Insurance Company's new seven-story office building, located at 1935 South Main Street, was designed in the International Style by the architects Slack W. Winburn and his son David Winburn. The structure was designed as "steel and porcelainized," following the precedent at the First Security Bank Building, according to the August 25, 1957, *Salt Lake Tribune.* The building was constructed by Williams and Peterson Contractors. Surety Life planned to occupy the lower three floors while leasing out the top four. Coming in at a cost of $1.25 million, Lewis T. Ellsworth, Surety president, said at the dedication in 1957 that the building is "a monument to opportunity and to American free enterprise." Consisting of two volumes, the main massing of seven stories was bookended by blocks that extended vertically beyond the main form, which was punctuated with long ribbon windows. Though really a simple rectangular form, the Winburns mastered the solid and void facade with ease. The south-facing windows of the main block were all outfitted with continuous aluminum sunshades. The main level extended to the south in a bar that mirrored the larger volume, and the entry was emphasized with a long, cantilevered canopy. (Courtesy USHS.)

BEEHIVE STATE BANK, 1961. Beehive State Bank was the anchor tenant on the main level of the 94,000-square-foot, eight-story building financed by oilman Col. D. Harold Byrd of Dallas, Texas. The new structure would replace the landmark E.B. Wicks Company Building (1937), pictured above. The Wicks Company Building was a fine example of the International Style in Salt Lake, though on a small scale. The architects of Beehive State Bank were Harwood K. Smith Partners of Dallas, Texas, and Jackson and Sharp of Salt Lake City. As reported in the June 12, 1960, Salt Lake Tribune, the first floor of the structure would be "entirely glass enclosed" and "the new structure will be built of reinforced concrete and steel with glass curtain walls and porcelainized steel on the north and south of the building." The interiors would be finished in walnut and bronze. The bank moved into the new offices officially on October 9, 1961, amid ceremonies attended by Utah's governor George Clyde and Salt Lake City mayor J. Bracken Lee and was marketed as the "most beautiful bank in the Mountain West." The Hercules Powder Company secured the lease on the remaining seven floors in the new building as its operations expanded with increased orders within the Minuteman intercontinental ballistic missile (ICBM) program. The design of the Beehive State Bank was a diluted version of the International Style reduced to a spare box, the main level embellished with storefront glass, the north and south facades filled with ribbon windows, and the east and west facades were solid brick. (Both, courtesy USHS.)

International Business Machines, 1962. International Business Machines Corporation (IBM) called for bids in July 1960 for its modern, four-story, half-million-dollar branch headquarters building at the intersection of South Temple Street and East Third Avenue. The architects were James Hunter & Associates of Boulder, Colorado, with Donald H. Panushka and Associates of Salt Lake City as the associate architects. The unique building featured repeating barrel-vaulted ceilings of "post-stressed concrete construction which extended through the north and south facades framing an expansive window wall, the effect of which allowed one to see into the interior of the barrel vaulted building. The interiors were painted white with 'certain wall areas and doors . . . painted either a brilliant orange or blue,' " reported the December 17, 1961, *Salt Lake Tribune*. The east and west walls were faced with a cast stone. The first two floors housed IBM's offices with the basement housing "shop and repair service, parts and supplies, classroom and employe [sic] lunchroom." The dedication was attended by civic leaders, including the mayor of Salt Lake, J. Bracken Lee, and Gov. George D. Clyde, who cut the ribbon. The project, constructed by Alfred Brown Co. at a cost of $900,000, was opened in January 1962. An open house was held that same month and had on display the IBM 1401 Data Processing System among other computing machines, including the 632 Electronic Typing Calculator, which "types, adds and multiplies," noted the January 24, 1962, *Salt Lake Tribune*. (Courtesy USHS.)

KENNECOTT BUILDING, 1965. Zions Securities Corporation, the financial arm of the Church of Jesus Christ of Latter-day Saints, announced the construction of a new office tower in 1959, and although discussion had been ongoing by that time, bidding on the project would be delayed until 1962. The joint venture of Garff, Ryberg, and Garff Construction and Okland Construction were the low bidders ($8.324 million) on the ambitious project at the southeast corner of Main Street and South Temple Street. The 334,525-square-foot, 18-story Kennecott Building was completed in 1965 and was so named for the role the Kennecott Copper Corporation played in the industrial development of Utah's modern economy. (Courtesy USHS.)

TEMPLETON BUILDING, 1890.
Named for its close proximity to
the Salt Lake Temple, the stately
Templeton Building, a six-story
brick and stone structure designed
by Joseph Don Carlos Young,
son of Mormon prophet Brigham
Young, was demolished to make
way for the new copper tower.
The new Kennecott Building
was clad in 600,000 pounds of
porcelainized copper sheathing,
mined and refined in Utah, and
was the world's largest copper-
sheathed structure. The porcelain
glaze was intended to retain
"copper's colorful characteristics,"
according to the September 23,
1962, *Salt Lake Tribune*. It was built
on structural steel piles driven 70
feet below ground, said to "resist
earthquakes and 100-mile per
hour winds." The building was
designed by the firm of Ashton,
Evans & Brazier Architects of Salt
Lake City. (Courtesy USHS.)

UNIVERSITY CLUB, 1965. By the
1960s, the property value of
the old University Club, being
close to downtown and on the
venerable South Temple Street,
was on the rise, and the club
began planning for a large-
scale redevelopment of the site.
The planned building would
be Utah's tallest at 24 floors,
16 of which would be used as
office space. There would also
be one floor of commercial at
the street level and five floors of
parking, and the top floors were
to house the new University
Club. (Courtesy USHS.)

OLD UNIVERSITY CLUB, 1904. The old University Club building (1904), located at 136 East South Temple Street, and the neighboring Keith Hotel would be razed to make way for the new structure. The University Club entered into an agreement with Bloomfield Building Industries of Memphis, Tennessee, who purchased the land, constructed the building, and then leased the top two floors back to the University Club for a term of 48 years. The structural frame was topped off in December 1964. Architect Ashley T. Carpenter, of Carpenter and Stringham Architects, estimated the cost at about $6 million. (Courtesy USHS.)

UNION PACIFIC BUILDING, 1966. Plans were drawn up for a $1.5-million face-lift of the old Deseret News Building, pictured on the next page, beginning in 1965 by George Cannon Young of Deseret Architects and Engineers. Horne-Zwick Construction Company was the contractor, and when complete, the building would have a new exterior of "polished granite and cast aggregate stone," noted the January 15, 1965, *Deseret News*, and have one additional floor added. The modernized structure respected the original building by maintaining the fenestration patterns in the new facades, though with more verticality than the original. Though demolished, the building that stands there now has maintained the chamfered corner of the original Richard Kletting–designed building. (Courtesy USHS.)

DESERET NEWS BUILDING, C. 1910. The decorated, brown-stone clad, six-story Deseret News Building at the corner of South Temple and Main Streets was designed by German-born Richard K.A. Kletting, the famed Utah architect known for designing the Utah State Capitol. The structure was marketed as a "fireproof" building, and Kletting was an innovator in the use of modern construction methods of the time with "cement floors throughout, iron pillars encased in cement, iron beams, iron stairs," according to the February 10, 1900, *Deseret Evening News*. The Deseret News Building was constructed by Soren Jacobsen (1881–1962), whose construction legacy continues to this day. Jacobsen died in 1962, and the building he constructed was, by the early 1960s, outmoded. (Courtesy USHS.)

LDS ADMINISTRATION BUILDING, 1972. George Cannon Young, whose architectural pedigree was storied—his father being Joseph Don Carlos Young and his grandfather Brigham Young—designed the skyscraping headquarters for the expanding global church. Church administration was scattered throughout the city in 13 separate office buildings, and this project would centralize the administrative functions. The planned building would be erected over a three-story underground parking structure, which was completed in 1965 in advance of the tower. The low bid came in at $31 million by the joint venture of Christiansen Brother Inc. and W.W. Clyde and Co. (Courtesy USHS.)

LDS Administration Building, Materials. The office tower was to be the tallest in Utah and would be faced with a precast white quartzite stone panel inspired by the iconic temple to the west. Topping out at 28 stories, the building's last girder was placed in early 1971. The approximately 1,000 concrete panels supplied by the Otto Buehner Company were intended as sunshades, each one being 30 feet long. The building featured an east and west wing, each four stories with cast-stone relief panels facing North Temple and the plaza to the south. Each of the four panels was 64 feet long and 33 feet high, weighing 60 tons. The relief panels on the west wing featured the western hemisphere and those on the east wing the eastern hemisphere. At 420 feet, with 21 elevators and 3,600 windows, the building enclosed 683,000 net square feet of office space, which would accommodate 1,900 church employees. The lobby space was finished in terrazzo flooring; stained wood paneling; and an impressive oil mural by artist Grant Romney Clawson (1927–2016), a copy of Harry Anderson's 1964 painting depicting the resurrected Savior commissioning His 11 apostles to go and teach all the nations. The building was dedicated on July 24, 1975. Lewis Nielsen, the building administrator, described the structure at the time as functional and built to last. (Courtesy USHS.)

ZIONS FIRST NATIONAL BANK BRANCH, 1963. The Cannon-Papanikolas Construction Company was awarded the $69,900 contract to erect a branch bank building for Zions First National Bank at 800 West and 2100 South. The new branch would have a unique vaulted roof and, with its west-side location, would fill a growing need as businesses were locating to the nearby Wagner Industrial Park. The new branch was designed by Ashton, Evans & Brazier Architects and was part of a trend by Zions First National Bank to establish branches throughout the Salt Lake Valley. (Both, courtesy USHS.)

Zions First National Bank Branch, 1964. The extraterrestrial bank building at 400 South and 700 East made its landing in the summer of 1964 and was designed by local architects Ashton, Brazier, Montmorency & Associates and constructed by the Bowers Construction Company at a cost of $108,000. This branch was Zions's eighth bank in the area and further continued the trend of establishing branches in the Salt Lake Valley. The circular bank building was specifically designed to serve automobile traffic, which allowed cars to drive around the structure and through the drive through. Described as a modernistic, round building, the dedication was anachronistic; girls adorned in "pioneer dress" passed around servings of sponge cake and a stagecoach "thundered up to the doors of the very modern structure," unloading bags of replica 1873 pioneer money, reported the June 26, 1964, *Deseret News and Salt Lake Telegram*. The dedication ceremonies were presided over by Elder Delbert L. Stapely of the Council of the Twelve Apostles, and on signal from Leland B. Flint, president of Zions, 300 guests "armed with scissors" cut the ceremonial 100-yard ribbon wrapped around the building. (Courtesy Steven Cornell.)

**PRUDENTIAL FEDERAL SAVINGS AND LOAN BUILDING,
1964.** Announced as "one of the garden spots of
downtown Salt Lake City" in the June 16, 1962,
Deseret News and Salt Lake Telegram, the $3-million,
five-story, 80,000-square-foot office building would
feature a 70-by-21-foot garden recessed two levels
below the street along with a full five-story atrium.
The upper floors surrounded a U-shaped atrium
space that opened onto Main Street behind a five-
story sculptural screen of more than 100 bronzed
seagulls in flight, sculpted by Tom Van Sant of
Los Angeles. The building was constructed by
Fullmer Brothers Construction. William L. Pereira
of Pereira and Associates of Los Angeles was the
design architect, and he created a sculpture in
and of itself. The structural system of the building
was unique to say the least—a steel and concrete
structure with two 81-ton steel girders resting on
columns flanking the east and west ends of the
atrium, allowing the main level to be completely
unobstructed from columns, while all the upper
floors were suspended from the massive roof
structure. A large skylight topped the atrium, and
the interiors were embellished with solid walnut
paneling, beige travertine marble, and a deep
blue soft-pile carpeting. (Both, courtesy USHS.)

DEMOLITION OF THE GLADSTONE AND ARMSTRONG BUILDINGS. The new Prudential Federal Savings and Loan Building was constructed just north of the existing Prudential office at 125 South Main Street and would require the demolition of the Gladstone and Armstrong Buildings. Each floor of the new structure (previous page) was given a different color theme, and the garden level housed the employees' cafeteria and lounge. Pereira's design was so un-building-like it appeared almost unfinished with the steel structure (protected in concrete) expressed architecturally on the exterior of the building. Pereira himself described the result as "reminiscent of the delicate spires and flying buttresses of the Gothic period," as reported in the July 3, 1962, *Salt Lake Tribune*. (Courtesy USHS.)

STEINER-AMERICAN BUILDING, 1967. Designed by William Browning of the firm Scott, Louie & Browning, the Steiner-American Corporation, a commercial linen supply company, built its new half-million-dollar headquarters at 505 East South Temple Street. Built by the Cannon Construction Company, the entry to the 15,000-square-foot building was through the tower enclosed with four 26-foot-tall glass panels. A three-ton air-conditioner was installed to cool the Minneapolis Honeywell Model 200 Series 120 computer housed behind a glass screen. With the snip of a towel, an homage to the company's products, Gov. Calvin Rampton ceremonially opened the new building. Browning's use of brick as a vernacular material was intended to achieve a sensitive design within the historic context of South Temple. (Courtesy Steven Cornell.)

WIER-COSGRIFF MANSION, C. 1900. The site of the Steiner-American Building was formerly occupied by the Wier-Cosgriff Mansion, a neo-Classical mansion designed by Salt Lake architect Walter E. Ware at the turn of the century. The mansion's owner was Thomas Wier, a mining tycoon, and it was among the "stateliest of the many residences that ornamented the street," as described by Margaret D. Lester in *Brigham Street*. The house had 15 rooms and was another example of a stately mansion being demolished to make way for a modernist office building on the venerated street. (Courtesy USHS.)

THE DARLING BUILDING. The Darling Building, located on the corner of 300 South and Main Street, was formerly known as the J.R. and H.M. Walker Mercantile Building. Designed in the Victorian Romanesque style by Carroll and Kern Architects in 1891, it caught fire in 1969 as was eventually demolished to make way for the new J.C. Penney Building. (Courtesy USHS.)

J.C. PENNEY, 1971. Seen on the left side of the image, the J.C. Penney Building was designed by the firm of Scott, Louie, and Browning, and the $6-million, 15-story office building was constructed by Zions First National Bank for J.C. Penney's accounting offices. Again, Browning used brick as the primary material on the 202 feet of vertical facade to maintain congruence with the surrounding architecture. The project was underway by May 1970. The contractor was W.P. Harlin Construction Company. (Courtesy USHS.)

Four

INDUSTRIAL ARCHITECTURE

MOUNTAIN STATES TELEPHONE AND TELEGRAPH COMPANY (MST&T), 1911. Based in Denver, Colorado, the Mountain States Telephone and Telegraph Company formed when Colorado Telephone, Tri-State Telephone, and Rocky Mountain Bell merged in 1911. The MST&T offices in Salt Lake City were located at 54–56 South State Street, just to the north of the Salt Lake Theater. Originally built in 1893 as a three-story building for Rocky Mountain Bell and designed by Richard Kletting, it was expanded to five floors in 1904. The Telephone Building was constructed of reinforced concrete and clad in a Romanesque Revival stone and brick facade. (Courtesy USHS.)

MST&T, 1940. Growth of the telephone was steady, and a $500,000 building was planned in Salt Lake City at 100 South State Street to house MST&T's main offices and provide space for telephone equipment. The building had a full basement and three stories but was designed to accommodate five additional stories. Its design was a "modern classic style" faced with terra-cotta. The main floor was the business office "designed for the convenience of the public," according to the January 10, 1939, *Salt Lake Tribune*. Excavation was started in March 1939, and by December, the offices on the main floor were open. The bronze doors were manufactured by the Cincinnati Metalcraft Company. The structure was warmly received and awarded the Most Outstanding Building Award in 1940 by the Utah Chapter of the American Institute of Architects. Constructed by the J.R. Howell Construction Company of Denver, the local Salt Lake City firm of Ashton & Evans were the architects. (Courtesy USHS.)

SALT LAKE THEATER, 1862. The MST&T Building occupied the site of the famed Salt Lake Theater, built by the Mormon pioneers in 1862. Designed by William H. Folsom, the 1,500-seat theater cost $100,000 and was the largest building in Utah. Upon purchase by MST&T, it was razed in 1928. By March 1939, the last vestiges of the theater's foundation were removed to make way for the new building, which featured a bas-relief bronze sculpture designed and cast by Mahonri Mackintosh Young, grandson of Brigham Young, to memorialize the renowned theater. (Courtesy USHS.)

MST&T, 1946–1957. By 1946, the building needed to be enlarged due to the population increase brought on by the war, and the addition of three floors to the existing building along with a new six-story wing housing two new elevators to the north would "provide Salt Lake City with the most modern and efficient service facilities obtainable," according to manager Franklin Cundiff in the August 4, 1946, *Salt Lake Tribune*. The Civilian Production Administration managed the estimated $750,000 project, and Jacobsen Construction Company was the general contractor, with Ashton & Evans hired to design the project. Steel shortages delayed the project start as Jacobsen Construction Company waited on nine carloads of steel to complete the project. By the summer of 1947, the building was nearing completion. By 1956, another addition was being planned, this time a $5-million, 67,000-square-foot, three-story structure to the north of the building on State Street. The addition was constructed by the Christiansen Bros. Construction Co. and was to match the existing building with terra-cotta. Ashton, Evans & Brazier Architects were hired for the design. The L-shaped addition, though just three floors, was designed to accommodate another five floors if necessary. (Courtesy USHS.)

MST&T, EXPANSION DOWNTOWN. In September 1952, MST&T announced an office building construction program in downtown Salt Lake City that would consist of two structures on the northwest corner of 100 South and 300 East. Ashton, Evans & Brazier were selected as the architects, and in November 1952, the Jacobsen Construction Company began work on the $300,000 project. The project included a larger building facing the corner that would house the accounting offices of the company, which had remained in the old Telephone Building on State Street, and a smaller one-story structure set behind to house the coin-counting operations. (Courtesy USHS.)

MST&T, 1970s. By 1968, MST&T's expansion was exponential, and plans were announced for a new, $5-million, 200,000-square-foot data processing building on the corner of 200 South and 200 East. The new structure would permit the expansion of telephone switching equipment. The design of the austere structure by Folsom and Hunt Architects and Engineers was built by Tolboe Construction Company, and the design could accommodate an additional nine stories, according to Eric Aaberg, vice president and general manager. The aggressive expansion foretold another big change, that of modernizing the name of the company to Mountain Bell. The site of the new building was formerly occupied by the First Presbyterian Church (1874), pictured above. By March 1971, the new offices were complete. The four-story structure was largely windowless but was embellished with twin bronze sculptures by Salt Lake sculptor Angelo Caravaglia. Additional floors were later added, seen in the image below (Above, courtesy USHS; below, courtesy Steven Cornell.)

MOUNTAIN FUEL SUPPLY COMPANY (MFSC), 1957. MFSC began in 1928 as the oil and gas exploration and production division of Western Public Service Corporation, a Salt Lake City holding company serving the Salt Lake Valley with natural gas from northern Utah and southwestern Wyoming. MFSC began planning for a multistoried office building at the southwest corner of 200 East and 100 South in 1954. By December 1957, the company was occupying the four-story, 70,000-square-foot headquarters. Exuding energy efficiency, the building was heated by natural gas and featured "sun-resistant" windows, two panes with a louver sandwiched between. The design of the L-shaped building could accommodate three additional stories should future growth require it. The steel-frame building was clad in a "red granite at street level and green porcelainized steel with aluminum trim on upper floors," according to the May 5, 1957, *Salt Lake Tribune.* Hodgson and Holbrook Architects and Engineers of Ogden designed the $1.9-million building. Tolboe and Harlin Construction Company was the general contractor. (Courtesy USHS.)

UTAH POWER AND LIGHT, 1912. Utah Power and Light (UP&L) was organized in 1912 as a conglomerate of smaller individually owned electric utilities. It eventually acquired 130 companies and was the primary electric utility for Utah. UP&L occupied the former Tribune Building at 133 South West Temple, and once it too was consolidated, UP&L moved into this building. (Courtesy USHS.)

THE UTAH LIGHT AND TRACTION COMPANY (UL&TC). UL&TC was one of the smaller conglomerates acquired by UP&L. The UL&TC built an extensive network of electric-powered streetcars throughout the city in the early 20th century, and the company constructed its carbarns between 500 and 600 South on 700 East in 1908. The barns would later be adaptively reused in the early 1970s as the Trolley Square Shopping Center. (Courtesy USHS.)

UTAH POWER AND LIGHT, 1950S. As part of UP&L's five-year, $61-million expansion in the Intermountain region, in 1948, the company purchased 26.6 acres of land adjacent to its present Jordan plant on the west side of Salt Lake City, near the Jordan River. The first section of the Gadsby steam electric plant, capable of producing 66,000 kilowatts of electricity, estimated at a cost of $10 million, was planned to be in operation by the end 1951, with a second $12-million section, capable of producing 75,000 kilowatts, to follow in 1952. The new plant would utilize a form of fuel known as "pitch," a low-cost, low-grade residual fuel supplied by Standard Oil of California. (Courtesy USHS.)

UP&L, GADSBY PLANT. Three 250-foot-tall reinforced concrete smokestacks were the major features of the plant. Each section was to use an estimated 70,000 gallons of continuously recycled water per minute and replaced when evaporation loss occurred by water from the Jordan River. By the end of the expansion phase, the three sections cost $38 million and were capable of generating 241,000 kilowatts of electricity. George Gadsby, president of UP&L, was venerated in January 1951 when officials announced the company's new steam plant would bear his name. Gadsby, a 21-year veteran of the company, guided UP&L through the Depression and subsequent war. (Courtesy USHS.)

UP&L, OFFICES. In 1951, the Jacobsen Construction Company began constructing the new $1-million ultra-modern operations center located at 1359 West North Temple Street. Described in the July 22, 1951, *Salt Lake Tribune* as having a "challenging appearance to motorists on the airport road," the facility, designed by Ashton, Evans & Brazier Architects, was heated and cooled by the heat generated at the new Gadsby Plant. The drafting room provided maximum light by slanted, colored glass windows on the North Temple Street side and by overhead glass in the ceiling. By 1958, another 70,000 square feet of office space was under construction for UP&L by the Alfred Brown Co. of Salt Lake. The new structure was located just west of the operations center and would be connected physically and architecturally. (Courtesy USHS.)

FISHER BREWING, 1884–1934. Albert Fisher was born in Germany in 1852 and immigrated to the United States in the 1870s. Upon starting the Albert Fisher Brewing Company in 1884, he bought 15 acres of land on the Jordan River and began construction of his Victorian-era brewery. In 1917, when the Eighteenth Amendment was proposed by Congress (ratified in 1919), Fisher Brewing closed its doors. With the repeal of the Prohibition in 1933, Fisher Brewing began to prepare for production in the spring of 1934. (Courtesy USHS.)

FISHER BREWING, 1946–1952. The Depression years and World War II would significantly impact the growth of the operation, but by 1946, Fisher Brewing was expanding its enterprise with a $1-million, three-phase modernization upgrade that included a bottling house, a storage facility, and a brewing house. The brewing house was to accommodate a "new all-copper kettle" that was fabricated in Europe. The architects for the project were Wohlob and Wohlob of Olympia, Washington, and Ashton, Evans & Brazier of Salt Lake City. (Courtesy USHS.)

FISHER BREWING, THE BREWING HOUSE. Located at 200 South and 1000 West, the new facilities had a distinctly Bauhaus flair. Facing 100 South, the southeast corner of the building gave way to a window wall, putting the brewing operation on full display. The boxy, rectangular buildings were designed to the utmost functional purpose, housing the modern manufacturing within. The

new, modern facilities wrapped in front of the former Victorian building, which remained from the original brewery, and Fisher Brewing began advertising beer that was "Made in America's Most Modern Brewhouse." (Courtesy USHS.)

PACIFIC NORTHWEST PIPELINE BUILDING, 1958. The 8.5-story Pacific Northwest Pipeline (PNP) Building, at the northeast corner of 200 South and 300 East, was to be the headquarters for the company that managed the Pacific-Northwest Pipeline, a 1,847-mile pipeline that would transport natural gas to the Intermountain area and the Pacific Northwest. Salt Lake City was selected as the headquarters due to its central location amid PNP's vast pipeline network. The 95,000-square-foot porcelainized steel structure was completed in 1958 at a cost of $2.5 million. The building followed closely on the heels of the First Security Bank Building and was also designed in the International Style, attempting to replicate the volumetric massing of its elder sibling but with less architectural skill, relying more on material and color changes. The building is largely a rectangular block with a projecting canopy defining the one-story base, a vertical frame at the east end of the main facade defining the entry, and a projecting stair tower on the east. The half-story is made by the inset extrusion on the roof. The rear facade is largely flat. The ribbon windows give each successive story a sense of weightlessness. The south-facing windows were outfitted with aluminum sunshades. The building contained such features as: "three high speed automatic elevators, cafeteria for employees on the main floor, air-conditioning and filtering," according to the February 3, 1957, *Salt Lake Tribune*. Fifty percent of the building skin was covered in heat-resistant glass in aluminum-framed windows. Slack W. Winburn and his son David, prominent local architects, were the designers of the building. The structure was located near the new building for the Mountain Fuel Supply Co., PNP's principal local customer. (Courtesy USHS.)

Five

HOTEL, MOTEL, AND APARTMENT ARCHITECTURE

HOTEL UTAH MOTOR LODGE, 1958. A new breed of hotels began with the $3-million Hotel Utah Motor Lodge, which was unique with its five angled concrete pylons forming the porte cochere. The auditorium and exhibit hall were distinctive features of the new motel, which allowed one to drive into the basement, where the 1,300-seat auditorium and football field–length exhibit hall were located. (Courtesy USHS.)

HOTEL UTAH MOTOR LODGE, BUILDERS AND ARCHITECTS. The project was constructed by the Jensen Construction Company. Constructed adjacent to Temple Square on the northwest corner of North Temple and West Temple Streets, its 154 rooms were a convenient walk to the sacred grounds. The designer was Cedar City–based architect L. Robert Gardner. Though modern in design, it was meant to harmonize with the Hotel Utah with its white, cast stone veneer. (Courtesy UUSC.)

HOTEL UTAH, 1960. When the new church administration building was announced in 1960, the old 10-story Hotel Utah, constructed in 1910, was included in the masterplan. A new addition was to be erected north of the present building and would be 10 stories, with a central tower reaching 17 stories, adding 300 additional rooms. Harold W. Burton, supervising church architect, stated the addition was planned because "the hotel is the best in Salt Lake City . . . and this will make it that much better," as the October 7, 1960, *Salt Lake Tribune* reported. The remodeled structure, though ultimately unbuilt, would have been stripped of its iconic classical detail and replaced with a somewhat featureless materiality in the new modern structure. (Courtesy USHS.)

TRI-ARC TRAVEL LODGE, 1970. Pearson Enterprises unveiled plans for the $3.3-million, 270-room, nine-story Travel Lodge in 1969. The Tri-Arc Travel Lodge boasted a "tri-arc" triangular design, which allowed each of the rooms to have an outside view with hotel services in the center, a design resulting from research by Travelodge Enterprises Inc. and the general contractor, the Austin Company of New Jersey. The innovative design sat atop a "mat" foundation containing 100 tons of steel rebar and over 1,700 cubic yards of concrete. The hotel was home to the new Utah Stars professional basketball team, who in their first year in Utah in 1971 won the ABA championship in a decisive Game 7 over the Kentucky Colonels, 131-121, in front of a capacity crowd of 13,260 at the Salt Palace. The Tri-Arc opened with a grand ceremony in June 1970 with Gov. Cal Rampton on hand. (Courtesy Steven Cornell.)

ROYAL INN, 1972. In 1971, the Royal Inn Hostelries broke ground on its new 200-room, 12-story Royal Inn at 200 South and West Temple Street, just south of the newly completed Salt Palace. On hand at the groundbreaking was the founder and chairman of Royal Inn Hostelries, Earl Gagosian, a native of Price, Utah. The company boasted the structure would be complete in five months, a result of its in-house architecture and engineering department. It actually opened on July 7, 1972, and filled a need, one that still resonates today, for convention goers at the Salt Palace. It was built of steel and faced with split-face block and brass trim, which "reinforces the clean image of Salt Lake City," according to the July 21, 1972, *Salt Lake Tribune*. Its distinctive curved balconies and exterior glass elevators were a novelty for Salt Lake. (Courtesy Steven Cornell.)

DOOLY BLOCK, 1891–1893. The Royal Inn would occupy the site on which the Dooly Block once stood. Designed by famed architect Louis Sullivan's firm, Adler and Sullivan, the six-story Dooly Block was a subdued version of the ornately rich organic style for which Sullivan was famous. The Dooly Block was razed in 1964 by owner Verne McCullough, and at the time, he had "no plans for the property . . . than to pave the cleared area to keep the dust down," reported the August 29, 1964, *Salt Lake Tribune*. (Courtesy USHS.)

HOWARD JOHNSON HOTEL, 1973. Another hotel project near the Salt Palace and Temple Square, the Howard Johnson Motor Lodge and Restaurant, a 228-room, 13-story hotel with a four-tier parking garage at 122 West South Temple Street, was started in 1972. Designed by the James Stewart Co. of Phoenix and Dean Gustavson Associates of Salt Lake City, the tower innovated the use of a high-strength steel, which negated the need for interior columns and footings. M. Seth Horne, a native of Utah, developed the $5.2-million hotel, which marketed itself to skier groups, tourists, salesmen, conventioneers, and large families. Construction began with the demolition of the Marion Hotel with Horne, Gov. Calvin Rampton, and Mayor Jake Garn wielding sledgehammers and hardhats. The new hotel opened in 1973. (Courtesy USHS.)

SALT LAKE HILTON, 1975. The Salt Lake Hilton, at 50 West and 500 South, was the third in line in the new convention hotels popping up on the west side of Salt Lake, although this one was balanced on the edge of downtown and the west side. The project began in 1973, when the $13-million hotel with 10 stories and 358 rooms was planned. It was touted as being a local hotel—locally owned by Robert Condie and Calvin Clark, designed by local architect Ron Molen, constructed by local contractor John Price & Associates, and run by locals. Image was everything apparently as the local Grower's Market was razed to make way for this project (pictured below). The locals got into some financial trouble, and the project was eventually purchased by Pearson Enterprises, owners of the local Tri-Arc Hotel. The Salt Lake Hilton was a building of "concrete, steel, iron and masonry." The hotel boasted 12 meeting rooms, with the largest, the Three Seasons Banquet Room, seating 830 people. However, it was the lobby that was the central feature of the hotel, with a "large, sunken conversational area in the center," according to the November 8, 1974, *Salt Lake Tribune.* The rooms facing the pool were listed as lanai rooms, with the second and third floors designated as suites, all with either a "heart, Grecian motif, half-circle and full clover" tub. The more conventional 200 tower rooms above all had "a view of the city and surrounding mountains." (Above, courtesy Steven Cornell; below, courtesy USHS.)

BEN ALBERT APARTMENTS, 1950. The $700,000, seven-story Ben Albert Apartments, located downtown at 130 South and 500 East, were the brainchild of Ben Davis and A.P. "Albert" Neilson. Its name derived from its owners' names, Ben and Albert. Comarketed along with the Ben Aire Apartments, its garden-style sibling around the corner, the Ben Albert was "close to downtown Salt Lake—yet far enough away to avoid the confusion and activity," reported the September 11, 1949, *Salt Lake Tribune*. Designed by architect Slack Winburn, the building was constructed of a steel and concrete skeleton yet faced with brick and terra-cotta to break up the ultra-modern block. The Ben Albert Apartments were completed in the fall of 1950 and were the first serious foray into the International Style by a local architect. (Courtesy USHS.)

GEORGIA APARTMENTS, 1950. Located at 200 East and 2100 South, the 46-unit, E-shaped Georgia apartments were to be an "apartment house of modernistic South American architecture," according to the January 22, 1950, *Salt Lake Tribune*. The brothers Papanikolas (Nick, John, and Gus) were the developers, and the brothers Wood (Charles and Roger) were the architects. The project was constructed by the Cannon-Papanikolas Construction Company and was built of cinderblock supplied by the Buehner Block Company. Built around garden courtyards, the projecting arms were two stories and the rear spine three stories. The E-shape opened toward the west along 200 East, which "affords maximum utilization of sunlight" and was intended to serve "professional persons and others in the vicinity of the Salt Lake County hospital." The project was completed in 1951. An "identical Latin style structure" was erected by the same builders in Provo, Utah. (Courtesy USHS.)

THE CHARLESTON, 1951. Construction on the L-shaped Charleston Apartments, just below the University of Utah on the northwest corner of 1300 East and 500 South, began in 1949 with "earth sampling," an operation to determine the composition of the soils prior to construction, according to architect Slack Winburn. The apartment building was the largest of its kind in Utah. The design was the product of an architectural tour by its owner in Sweden and South America and helped to introduce the International Style to Utah. The 13-story, $1.5-million project was owned by Charles Peterson, and because of its steel reinforced concrete construction, he claimed in the December 17, 1950, *Salt Lake Tribune* that it would be "protected from the effects of an atomic bomb." The interior decoration was similarly bombproof, with the underside of the concrete floor slab as the finished surface, albeit painted, though the architect demurred and suggested that it was all done for seismic resistance. (Courtesy USHS.)

UNIVERSITY HEIGHTS, 1952. The University Heights Apartments, located at 130 South and 1300 East, were completed in 1952 by the Plewe Construction Company at a cost of $1 million. Designed by Scott and Beecher Architects, the eight-story, L-shaped building was constructed of a steel frame with brick veneer walls. The building was severely modern with punched window openings offering the only reprieve from the planar walls. The L-shaped plan allowed for the existing building on the corner to remain. (Courtesy USHS.)

University Heights, 1952. The sculptural canopied entry on ground level featured a series of arched concrete ribs extending from the entry out over the U-shaped driveway. Located west of the university, the project was to "serve the needs of the University of Utah and the new veterans hospital," according to the June 10, 1950, *Deseret News*. (Courtesy USHS.)

University Village, 1960. The $3-million housing project was built by Tolboe and Harlin Construction Company on the corner of Wasatch Drive and Sunnyside Avenue for the University of Utah and included 23 two-story masonry buildings that housed 299 married students and their families. The complex, designed by Scott and Beecher Architects, would replace Stadium Village, a community of frame structures built after World War II that were planned for demolition. The new village surrounded a central park intended to be enjoyed by the student families living there. (Courtesy USHS.)

WASATCH TOWERS, 1961. Construction on the 10-story, $1-million apartment complex on the east bench at 1235 East 200 South began in late 1958. The Wasatch Towers were to be the first co-operative apartment house in Utah, a new idea in which "tenants would own shares of the structure proportionate to the size and location of their apartment," according to the October 19, 1958, *Salt Lake Tribune*. The steel, concrete, and glass structure was designed by architect Bruce McDermott and clad with a fine ceramic tile. The large inset balconies were designed to maximize views of the valley to the west and the Wasatch Mountains to the east. Because of this opportunity, the owner, James Moyle, said two penthouse floors were added to the plans following the start of construction. Moyle was profiled after its completion as a tenant of a bachelor apartment, a compact unit with exceptional interior design, and he is featured sitting contemplatively at his bookcase/desk combination. (Courtesy USHS.)

ALBEN APARTMENTS, 1963. The Alben Apartments at 1810 South Main Street was another project by Ben Davis and A.P. Neilson, and the name derived again from their own, just as it did on the Ben Albert Apartments. The Alben was designed by Slack Winburn and Arthur K. Olsen at a cost of $2.4 million. Completed in 1963, it was a six-story, 174-unit apartment house that featured a "coffee shop, barber and beauty shops, variety store, lounge, swimming pool and sundeck," as reported in the August 25, 1963, *Salt Lake Tribune*. The Alben was innovative in its plan; it was a double-loaded U-shaped building with a center court containing a swimming pool and a putting green. (Courtesy USHS.)

ALBEN APARTMENTS, BUILT FOR SENIORS. The Alben was designed and built for seniors. The Alben Apartments received a $2-million Federal Housing Administration (FHA) loan for construction, but it was foreclosed on in 1966 by the FHA and put up for sale. Built exclusively for seniors, it appeared to have a high vacancy rate, and the terms of the mortgage were altered to allow for others to rent apartments there as long as seniors were given priority. The explanation for the foreclosure was that there was an excess supply of apartments built in Salt Lake City in the early 1960s, and vacancies were high. This was the first of many foreclosures by the FHA. The others to follow were the Sunset and Bonneville Towers. (Courtesy USHS.)

LANAI APARTMENTS, 1963. The 40-unit, five-story Lanai Apartments, at the southwest corner of 1100 East and 300 South and built for $800,000 by a pair of Denver-based developers, Arthur Friedman and Donald Gordon, was designed by Denver architect Leon Brim with the local firm of Scott and Louie acting as associate architects. The Lanai was named for the architectural element from Hawaii, which was essentially a roofed porch. (Courtesy USHS.)

OAK CREST GARDENS, 1963. Completed in 1963, the Oak Crest Gardens was located at the mouth of Emigration Canyon at 900 Donner Way. The building was owned by the R.D. Sawyer Investment Co., built by R.D. Sawyer Construction Co. of steel, concrete block, and glass, and designed by Ashton, Evans & Brazier Architects. Set high above the valley floor, each soundproof and fireproof unit had a porch extending across the entire building. The co-operative apartment building, the first large structure constructed under the new Utah condominium law, was a seven-story, $1.5-million project and consisted of two buildings connected by four-story sections with parking, apartments, and "a fallout-shelter, believed to be the first ever built into an apartment here," according to the October 13, 1963, *Salt Lake Tribune*. The project featured a lift-slab construction, which required that the steel structure was first erected and then "precast concrete floors will be jacked up one by one and welded into place," reported the October 28, 1962, *Salt Lake Tribune*. (Courtesy USHS.)

IRVING HEIGHTS, 1964. The Irving Heights apartments, at 1963 South 1200 East in Sugar House, were originally announced in 1961 as a 54-unit, five-story project financed by the Hogle Investment Company and designed by Verl Gessel of Ogden and Alma Jaeger of Salt Lake. By the end of 1962, however, it had increased to seven stories with 64 units, and the design had been drastically altered by architect Paul Lemoine of Salt Lake with "the first floor of the steel and reinforced modern concrete structure be devoted to shops, professional offices and a spacious lobby, on entrance," wrote the December 7, 1962, *Salt Lake Tribune*. Jacobs Construction was the contractor as well as one of the investors. The project opened in 1964. (Courtesy USHS.)

AZTEC APARTMENTS, 1965. Located at 503 South 1000 East, the Aztec was a 12-story structure with 72 apartments and two penthouses, along with a swimming pool and lounge and a "lanai for year 'round recreation including shuffleboard, and golf practice putting," above a two-story, below-grade parking garage, reported the February 16, 1964, *Salt Lake Tribune*. The "home in the sky" condominiums were "Salt Lake City's first all-electric skyrise" and were marketed for $19,390. Perched atop the bench, they hugged the edge of the University of Utah campus while being only a "five-minute drive from downtown." The apartments were styled in the clean, boxy confines of modernism but were embellished by architect William Rowe Smith's balcony railings and window spandrels with an Aztec-inspired motif. (Courtesy Steven Cornell.)

SUNSET TOWER, 1965. Sunset Tower was the first of three planned 15-story high-rise apartment houses by the Artcol Corporation, along with the Bonneville Towers and the Plaza Towers, all to be located downtown. The Plaza Towers were never built after the Artcol Corporation defaulted on the FHA-backed loans. The $2.7-million Sunset Tower, located at 40 South 900 East, was designed by local architect M.E. Harris and constructed by the Alfred Brown Company. It was marketed as "Fireproof and Earthquake proof" with an innovative inner-outer lobby that the developers claimed was the "most beautiful lobby in the city." The inner-outer lobby was simply an intercom system that allowed the tenant to "buzz" visitors in. The 15th floor featured penthouse units with "private garden terraces and a sweeping view of the valley and mountains." The massing of the towers followed the strict rules of modernism with its boxy design and its expansive ribbon windows but then was embellished with subtle brick details that enhanced the stark facades. The base of the tower was further embellished with stone and a futuristic precast concrete entry canopy with barrel vaults and projecting ribs that mimic designs by Eero Saarineen in projects like the Trans World Airlines (TWA) terminal at New York City's Kennedy Airport. (Courtesy USHS.)

STANSBURY APARTMENTS, 1966. In 1964, a toothy trio (dentists E. Keith Lignell, Burton M. Todd, and Wendell E. Taylor) announced a 10-story, 69-unit apartment house called Sky-Rise at the southeast corner of 700 East and 200 South. The architects, Edwards & Daniels, utilized a unique "central core idea" in the brick and masonry structure. By locating the stairs and two high-speed elevators at the center, the length of corridors could be greatly reduced. The core was the first component built, followed by the steel framework, which allowed the concrete floors to be poured and cured at ground level and hoisted into place using a lift-slab construction method. Two floors of underground parking supported the building above. Each apartment had its own balcony, and all residents had access to a common swimming pool, sauna, tennis courts, and a sundeck. (Courtesy Steven Cornell.)

BONNEVILLE TOWERS, 1967. Construction of the 15-story, $4.1-million tower at 777 East South Temple Street, the second by Artcol Corporation, began in 1964. Artcol engaged local architect M.E. Harris with Harold A. Carlson from Los Angeles and Alfred Brown as the contractor. The design of the Bonneville is similar to Sunset Tower, with its boxy massing and ribbon windows, albeit with recessed inset balconies and subtle brick embellishments. The base of the tower was differentiated with precast concrete wall panels and a more subdued entry canopy. (Courtesy USHS.)

Six

DEPARTMENT STORES AND RETAIL ARCHITECTURE

KEITH-O'BRIEN COMPANY AND AUERBACH'S DEPARTMENT STORE. David Keith, a Utah mining magnate, co-owned the Silver King Mine in Park City with Thomas Kearns. Keith and W.M. O'Brien began the Keith-O'Brien Company (KOB) in 1902 and by 1903 had occupied the David Keith Building on Main Street. By 1912, the merchant scene had pivoted to the parallel State Street, and the KOB Company moved with it to its new building on the southwest corner of State Street and 300 South for larger and better-suited spaces for a department store. The new building was three stories with a basement. (Courtesy USHS.)

KNUTSFORD HOTEL. With the KOB move, 300 South was now saturated with department stores—Auerbach's in the old Knutsford Hotel (pictured above), KOB at one end, the Paris Company in the center, and Walkers on the other corner. This section was known as the "Great White Way" due to the electrical displays of Auerbach's and KOB, which caused the intersection to be as light as day. (Courtesy UUSC.)

BROADWAY ANNEX. By the 1920s, with business expanding, KOB expanded operations into the old Mission building next door. It would be called the Broadway Annex. (Courtesy USHS.)

MODERNIZING THE ANNEX. By the 1940s, the Broadway Annex would be the KOB Company's only home, and its old building by the corner would be occupied by Auerbach's. The Broadway Annex was remodeled in 1945 and opened in a "rainbow of colors" behind a transparent front and a modern facade, reported the August 26, 1945, *Salt Lake Tribune*. Five hundred colors were used to decorate each of the floors in different shades of solid pastels and were provided with daylight illumination from fluorescent lamps. (Courtesy USHS.)

KOB, SUGAR HOUSE. In 1952, the Keith-O'Brien Company opened its modern department store in Sugar House on the southeast corner of 1100 East and 2100 South, the site of the former Sugar Factory. The four-level, $1-million store contained 26,000 square feet of space. The exterior walls were of a buff-colored terra-cotta with "verde antique terrazzo" below the marquee, noted the November 14, 1952, *Salt Lake Tribune*. The new suburban shopping center was financed by the William H. McIntyre Company, built by the Cannon Construction Company, and designed by Clifford Evans. (Courtesy USHS.)

AUERBACH BUILDING.
In 1960, Auerbach's
covered its building
with over an acre of
cast stone panels, each
weighing more than a
ton and manufactured
by Otto Buehner
Company. The panels
were of Mayan design.
Architects Carpenter
& Stringham
designed the new
facade. Auerbach's
stayed in its "Big
Store" until 1979,
when it was sold to
Coordinated Financial
Services, headed
by Gary Sheets.
(Courtesy USHS.)

PARIS COMPANY, 1913. According to the February 4, 1897, *Salt Lake Herald*, the Paris Millinery Company was "launched into corporate existence" that year at 118 South Main Street yet by 1901 had relocated down the street to 262–266 South Main Street. By 1911, the Paris Company had purchased the Judge property on East Third Avenue, occupied by the Freed Furniture Co., with plans for a building, "modern in every respect," reported the December 31, 1911, *Salt Lake Herald Republican*. Louis Simon, president of the Paris Company, took an extensive trip to the east to study "modern types of department store buildings," per the January 12, 1912, *Salt Lake Telegram*, and by the spring of 1913, the company had completed its new home, the most striking feature being the immense glazed dome, which allowed shoppers to always "shop by daylight," noted the April 30, 1913, *Salt Lake Tribune*. (Courtesy USHS.)

Paris Company, 1939. By 1939, though the Paris Company's structure was just 25 years old, plans were underway to modernize the building again. The firm of Wooley and Evans was pegged to design a cladding system to drape over the existing facade, which consisted of a "new terra-cotta and glass brick exterior, baked enamel marquee and chrome steel trimmed display windows," according to the May 28, 1939, *Salt Lake Tribune*. (Courtesy USHS.)

Southeast Furniture, 1951. Southeast Furniture Company was established in 1925 and was located "southeast" of the city in Sugar House. In 1950, the company announced a modernization program that would completely reconstruct the facade with polished cast stone and recessed display windows. The Southeast Furniture building had completed a quarter-million-dollar remodel with covered and lighted sidewalks and a new side entrance allowing customers to enter the store from the new 100-car parking lot. The architects were Young & Ehlers with stonework executed by the Otto Buehner Company. (Courtesy USHS.)

SEARS ROEBUCK, 1947. Sears occupied the Walker Mercantile Building on Main Street and 300 South prior to erecting its modern store. The contract for the new store was awarded to the Jacobsen Construction Company in July 1945 with the caveat that it would not begin until the "work no longer will interfere with war supporting activities," according to the July 19, 1945, *Salt Lake Tribune.* The new store was to house 250,000 square feet on 800 South between State and Main Streets. Seven stores were rolled into one—wearables, auto accessories, building materials, appliances, farm equipment, home furnishings, and specialties. Ashton & Evans was hired to prepare plans and specs for "one of the first major postwar projects in the city." The $1-million building would have two floors above grade with a basement and was described in the November 20, 1945, *Salt Lake Tribune* as "modern but conservative" by store manager E.W. Jenkins. The main facade was set back from a 500-car parking lot along 800 South that was 460 feet in length. A total of 35,000 people "jostled and rubbed elbows" when the store opened for business in July 1947, reported the July 18, 1947, *Salt Lake Tribune.* The most interesting feature of the new ultra-modern store design was the 11 murals measuring 18 feet long by 5 feet high depicting historic Utah events. (Both, courtesy USHS.)

DINWOODEY FURNITURE COMPANY, 1961. After its previous store was destroyed by fire, the Dinwoodey Furniture Company erected a new, six-story, Victorian Romanesque building at 37 West 100 South in 1890. Dinwoodey's, established around 1857, was one of Utah's oldest pioneer-era companies and the second-oldest furniture company west of the Mississippi. The company would embark on an addition and remodel in 1960, building a two-story annex to the east and modernizing the facade of its Victorian store. The architects were Snedeker, Budd, Monroe, and Associates, and the contractor was the Cannon Construction Company. (Both, courtesy USHS.)

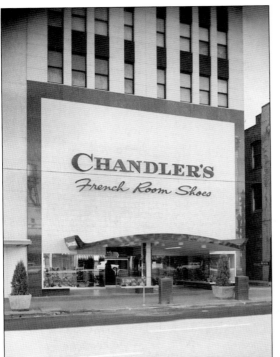

CHANDLER'S SHOE STORE, 1962. Operating in Salt Lake City since 1940, the large chain Chandler's, "French Room Shoes," with 440 stores in the United States, moved to its new home in the former Keith-O'Brien Broadway Annex building when its former site at 39 South Main Street was slated for demolition to make way for the new Zion's Co-operative Mercantile Institute (ZCMI) expansion. Chandler's occupied the lower and main levels and leased the upper floors to the Auerbach Company. Contemporary design marked the interior of the 8,000-square-foot store with "alternating panels of pewter foil and back lit translucent panels framed by charcoal leather," according to the August 18, 1962, *Salt Lake Tribune*. Chandler's architectural department in St. Louis designed the new spaces and facade. The interior was designed to have a "living room-salon atmosphere for casual shopping," reported the January 7, 1962, *Salt Lake Tribune*. (Both, courtesy USHS.)

ZCMI, 1975. Zion's Co-operative Mercantile Institute, known as "America's first department store," was founded in 1868 by Brigham Young as a means to establish an equitable business atmosphere. These co-ops were established in many early Mormon communities, but the flagship store was erected in 1876 on Main Street in Salt Lake City between South Temple Street and 100 South, and its elaborate cast iron facade was a symbol of its importance. In 1969, Zion's Securities Corporation announced plans for a major renewal of historic Block 75, bounded by Main Street, State Street, South Temple Street, and 100 South. The Main Street section of this block was still crowded with its 19th-century characters, but the northwest corner of the block had already undergone redevelopment with the demolition of the Templeton Building to make way for the 19-story Kennecott Building. Construction of the "largest enclosed downtown mall in the United States" was started in 1971, and as part of the $50-million redevelopment of the block, it was announced that two-thirds of ZCMI's historic cast-iron facade would be retained. The mall was serviced by a 2,000-car parking terrace and a 90,000-square-foot arcade. The principal tenant was ZCMI with a four-story, 427,000-square-foot space, which anchored the other 60 retailers, as well as a 27-story office tower. The project was largely seen as a necessity to beautify and modernize the downtown core. The massive project was designed by Gruen Associates of Los Angeles and was constructed by the joint venture of Christiansen Brothers and W.W. Clyde and Company. (Courtesy USHS.)

CROSSROADS PLAZA MALL, 1980. The redevelopment of Block 76, directly west of Block 75 and bounded by West Temple Street, Main Street, South Temple Street, and 100 South, was redeveloped in similar fashion for the construction of the Crossroads Plaza Mall in 1980. (Courtesy UUSC.)

Seven

EDUCATIONAL ARCHITECTURE

UNIVERSITY OF UTAH, 1945–1970. After World War II, as the GI Bill incentivized higher learning for returning American soldiers, enrollment reached record highs, and the need to expand the University of Utah campus became an urgent issue in the 1950s and 1960s. By the time of this 1972 photograph, the former campus nucleus of Presidents Circle had been vastly expanded upon, including the School of Medicine complex to the northeast (upper left); Sports and Special Events Center (middle right, including the Huntsman Center Dome); business, library, psychology, and classroom buildings (below the dome); a student union (immediately above Presidents Circle); and an engineering structure. Most of these new, modernist buildings were designed by members of the faculty at the University of Utah School of Architecture. The University of Utah's campus has continued to change dramatically over the last 50 years, with many of the facilities replaced by contemporary buildings with modern amenities as well as the addition of a research park south of Red Butte Creek. (Courtesy USHS.)

THE ANNEX, 1942. The Annex building was first constructed by the US Army for Fort Douglas during World War II and was donated to the University of Utah (along with the surrounding land) by order of Gen. Dwight Eisenhower in 1948 to provide needed classroom space during the postwar enrollment boom. While not architecturally modernist, the Annex represents the explosive growth of the university immediately following the war, which was eventually formalized in campus planning and a massive building program over the next 20 years. The Annex was demolished in 2021. (Courtesy UUSC.)

UNIVERSITY MEDICAL CENTER, 1951–1965. The university launched a four-year medical school program in 1943, though it was administered haphazardly through multiple campus buildings. With different structures coming online at various times, fundraising for the main building began in earnest in 1957, and eventually $16 million was raised through federal, state, and private sources. The University Medical Center included four structures: the main building (E-shaped with hospital, clinic, and College of Medicine wings); the Rehabilitation Building; the Cancer Research Building; and the Research Extension. The main building was designed by the local architectural firm of Ashton, Evans & Brazier. While the complex has continued to develop since its beginning, including a newer hospital and the Huntsman Cancer Center, most of the original University Medical Center remains. (Courtesy USHS.)

CANCER RESEARCH BUILDING, 1951. One of the first structures completed as part of the University Medical Center was the Cancer Research Building, constructed through funding from the US Public Health Service at a cost of $413,000. The four-story, 6,000-square-foot facility was designed by Ashton, Evans & Brazier Architects. (Courtesy USHS.)

SILL HOME LIVING CENTER, 1953. The Home Living Center was completed in 1953 by the Department of Home Economics and soon thereafter named after board of regents chair Sterling Sill, who championed its construction. The building was divided into small apartments so students could learn homemaking individually instead of the normal mode of instruction at the time, when students would learn in groups in a single, larger house. Ashton, Evans & Brazier Architects designed the $300,000 facility, one of the first on campus to be entirely funded through private donations. (Courtesy USHS.)

KENNECOTT RESEARCH CENTER, 1955. Kennecott Copper Corporation funded a research center to provide a bridge between engineers at the University of Utah and its mining operations on the west side of the Salt Lake Valley. The idea of a public-private partnership on campus was novel at the time, but it allowed the 50 employees of the company working in the building, most of whom held engineering degrees from the university, to connect with students in the classroom. (Courtesy USHS.)

ORSON SPENCER HALL, 1957. Lloyd Snedaker designed the classroom building that was named after Orson Spencer, the first chancellor of the University of Utah. A first phase opened in 1956, with an additional wing added to the project during construction. Despite construction delays, including a carpenters' strike while the addition was being framed, International Style Orson Spencer Hall opened on time for the 1957 fall semester for about $1.5 million (plus furnishings). Orson Spencer Hall served the university community for 60 years but was demolished in 2016 to make way for Gardner Commons. (Courtesy USHS.)

A. RAY OLPIN STUDENT UNION, 1959. Plans for a new union were approved in 1951 by a committee that had been formed about a year earlier to explore adding onto the existing student center. The old union's seven square feet per student was considered insufficient by 1950, when most unions had 12–20 square feet per student. Architect Fred L. Markham designed a modern facility to include all the amenities of a student hangout space. (Courtesy USHS.)

A. Ray Olpin Student Union. University president A. Ray Olpin led a groundbreaking ceremony for the union on May 27, 1954, after a few years of delays on the $2.5-million building, funded entirely from student fees. The union opened on New Year's Day 1957, with a modern cafeteria, movie theater, and music halls. The 10-lane bowling alley—featuring the first automatic pin-setting equipment in an American student union—opened with a separate ceremony led by Olpin in February. The union was eventually named after Olpin. (Courtesy USHS.)

MERRILL ENGINEERING BUILDING, 1959–1967. Architect Dean Gustafson designed the engineering building in 1959, and it was constructed in three main phases through the 1960s on the site of the former Fort Douglas golf course. With its wraparound glass curtain walls and simple rectangular form, the building represents the finest example of the International Style on the University of Utah campus and one of the purest examples of that style in Utah. Phase I was delayed by a strike of the Pittsburgh Plate Glass Company, which supplied the thousands of panes of glass required to enclose the building. The third and final phase of construction was completed in May 1967. (Courtesy USHS.)

UNIVERSITY BOOKSTORE, 1961. "New bookstore is now being used by Utes," announced the *Daily Utah Chronicle* on December 5, 1961. Woolley and Mohr designed the new campus building, constructed by M.B. McCullough at a cost of $390,000. The new bookstore replaced a smaller bookstore in the Park Building on Presidents Circle and offered self-service shopping, along with a small study area for students. The introduction of a "trade book area, an area of scholarly paperback books published by University presses and other publishers," including about 2,000 titles, was considered innovative at the time. While the bookstore still remains as a part of the campus store, it has been added onto, and the original form is not apparent from the exterior. (Courtesy USHS.)

LAW BUILDING, 1964. The new law building was opened with a May 1, 1964, lecture by Columbia law professor Walter Gellhorn titled, "A Decade of Desegregation: Retrospect and Prospect." The facility, which included classrooms, seminar rooms, an auditorium, and 300-seat courtroom, was design by a partnership of Lorenzo Young, Robert Fowler, and J. Shirl Cornwall. A low-slung, one-story wing included the instruction spaces, while a taller two-story volume included the law library, which itself cost over $1.25 million. (Courtesy USHS.)

BUSINESS BUILDING, 1963–1966. The School of Business joined in the mid-1960s building boom with a three-phase structure on the south side of campus. Phase I and II included the rectangular classrooms and faculty offices, while Phase III was a circular addition, including a 349-seat auditorium. The total cost of the three phases was $2 million. It was built by the Culp Construction Company and designed by architect William Rowe Smith. (Courtesy USHS.)

BIOLOGY BUILDING, 1968. A trio of science buildings were opened within a week of each other in May 1968, including the biology building. Hungarian biochemist Albert Szent-Gyorgyi, who won the 1937 Nobel Prize in Physiology or Medicine in part for isolating vitamin C, spoke at the building's dedication. (Courtesy USHS.)

EYRING CHEMISTRY BUILDING, 1968. The Eyring Chemistry Building was dedicated in May 1968 with a speech by Nobel Prize laureate George Porter, a British scientist who developed technology in molecular photography. The building cost $3.355 million to complete. As the *Daily Utah Chronicle* pointed out, "The extraordinary student population explosion necessitated an expansion of the University's physical facilities in recent years." (Courtesy USHS.)

FLETCHER PHYSICS BUILDING, 1968. A May 8, 1968, dedication ceremony of the new Fletcher Physics Building featured Dr. Frederick Seitz, president of the National Academy of Sciences. The building, eventually named after then president James C. Fletcher, was constructed at a cost of $2.2 million. The three separate volumes of the building were constructed for distinct functions in different styles (opaque research, transparent administration, and circular instruction) but were connected under one roof. (Courtesy Steven Cornell.)

SPORTS AND SPECIAL EVENTS CENTER, 1969. Now known as the Huntsman Center, the university began planning the Sports and Special Events Center (SEC) in the early 1960s as the inadequacies of the 5,000-seat Einar Nielsen Fieldhouse became apparent with a rising student population and more interest in attending sporting events beyond the campus community. The board of regents approved it in 1966. The centerpiece of the SEC, designed by Young and Fowler Associates, was a 15,000-seat arena, topped by what was the world's largest wood span dome at the time of construction (350 feet). The latticework of glue-laminated roof joists sat on a steel tension ring to minimize loads placed on its concrete base. (Courtesy UUSC.)

ADDITIONAL SEC FACILITIES. The $10.4-million complex also included a natatorium, fieldhouse, and three physical education buildings: West Building (specifically for female students), East Building (handball, volleyball, badminton, basketball, gymnastics, and weight lifting), and North Building (research, classrooms, volleyball, badminton, and basketball). The facility opened on November 21, 1969, with a dedication by Utah governor Calvin Rampton prior to a performance by comedian Bill Cosby. While the buildings have been upgraded over time, all five are still standing. (Courtesy UUSC.)

FINE ARTS CENTER, 1970. Brutalism made its appearance on the University of Utah campus with the construction of the $4-million, 144,700-square-foot Fine Arts Center, designed by Edwards & Daniels Architects. The center is comprised of four interconnected buildings: a museum and lecture hall, the Department of Art (now the College of Fine Arts), the Department of Architecture (now the College of Architecture and Planning), and sculpture. (Courtesy Steven Cornell.)

MARRIOTT LIBRARY, 1968. The *Utah Daily Chronicle* proudly boasted that the new library building "contains about 300,000 square feet of floor space—100,000 more than the new library at Brigham Young University, and large enough to accommodate nearly six football fields inside." Author Wallace Stegner dedicated the building on May 17, 1968. The New Formalist exterior featured floating solid volumes, contrasting with a light-filled central atrium. Another notable interior space was the Tanner Room, outfitted by O.C. Tanner with "gold-veined Mexican onyx, rich wood panelling, Barcelona chairs, and shades of green velvet." While the Marriott Library still stands, a seismic retrofit and expansion in 2009 watered down the aesthetic of the original Lorenzo S. Young design. (Courtesy USHS.)

WESTMINSTER COLLEGE, 1960–1969. Like the University of Utah, Salt Lake City–based Westminster College experienced a dramatic rise in student population through the 1950s and 1960s. Modern residence halls were built for women (Hogle Hall) in 1960, including a dining hall, and Carleson Hall was constructed for men in 1962. The administration building was completed in 1967 and was designed by the architectural partnership of Carpenter & Stringham. (Courtesy WUGL.)

HOGLE HALL, 1960. Construction on the women's dormitory was completed by the Jacobsen Construction Company in September 1960. The $500,000 residence hall housed 125 women and was meant to alleviate overcrowding in the historic Ferry Hall. US congressman David King was on hand for the ribbon cutting, along with Westminster president Dr. Frank Duddy Jr. Hogle Hall was named after James E. Hogle, also the namesake for Salt Lake's Hogle Zoo. (Courtesy WUGL.)

WALKER HALL, 1960. Walker Hall, with its distinct space-frame sawtooth roof, was originally built as the dining hall for Hogle Hall. It was originally anticipated to open in May 1960, but the construction was delayed as the delivery of 85-foot I beams from Bethlehem Steel fell prey to the steel strike of 1959. Walker Hall currently serves as the Center for Veteran and Military Services as well as for mail services. (Courtesy WUGL.)

NIGHTINGALE MEMORIAL LIBRARY, 1964. Nightingale Memorial Library was made possible by a grant from the Mountain Fuel Supply Company on behalf of its chairman, W.T. Nightingale, who died while the building was being constructed. Designed by Arne Purhonen and built by McDowell and Rapp, the structure was able to house over 50,000 books. Following the completion of Giovale Library in 1997, Nightingale was converted to the Bassis Center for Student Learning. (Courtesy WUGL.)

BAMBERGER HALL, 1967. Westminster College eased some of the cramped conditions in historic Converse Hall (1906) by building a new administration building, later named Bamberger Hall, in 1967. Designed by Carpenter & Stringham, Bamberger Hall originally contained 15,000 square feet of offices and three classrooms. The building was renovated in 2002 and still houses campus administrative staff. (Courtesy WUGL.)

CARLESON HALL, 1962. Built to complement the women's dormitory at Hogle Hall, the $450,000 men's dormitory was named after Fred and Harry Carleson, brothers who had a successful car dealership in Salt Lake and donated $25,000 to furnish the new structure. Originally, Carleson Hall housed 120 students in 53 double rooms and 14 singles. Both Hogle and Carleson Halls remain active dormitories, though they are now both coed. (Courtesy Steven Cornell.)

STUDENT UNION, 1969. The student union was completed in 1969 and named after Manford A. Shaw, university president at the time of its completion, when he retired in 1976. The building originally served as a student center, post office, and small recreation center, along with food service operations that were moved out of Walker Hall. A bookstore was added in 1982. The Shaw Student Center was renovated in 2001 and remains a center for campus activity. (Courtesy WUGL.)

JUDGE MEMORIAL HIGH SCHOOL, 1960. Judge Memorial High School was first opened in 1892 after the widow of Park City mining magnate John J. Judge built a miners' hospital on the east bench. It became a Catholic school in 1920, first as Cathedral High School, then as Judge Memorial High School starting in 1929. The old building was deemed unsatisfactory by the late 1950s, and a new modern high school was completed in time for the fall 1960 semester. The original Judge Memorial High School was demolished in 1966. (Courtesy Steven Cornell.)

HIGHLAND HIGH SCHOOL, 1956–1958. Highland High School was built on the site of the old state prison in modern-day Sugar House Park. The school was built in phases by Paulsen Construction Company and Alfred Brown Company at a cost just under $5 million. The classroom wing was completed in 1956, the gymnasium wing in the fall of 1957, and, by 1958, the shops and the auditorium wing were complete. Designed by architect Lorenzo Young, there was a bit of controversy over the 27-foot-tall pylon identifying the name of the school, some calling it unnecessary and a "wanton waste of taxpayer money" in the August 23, 1956, *Salt Lake Tribune*. (Courtesy USHS.)

HIGHLAND HIGH SCHOOL. As reported in the October 10, 1958, *Deseret News*, the new high school had "65 classrooms, including laboratories, a study hall, social room, library, teachers' room, bookstore, cafeteria, drafting room, two audio visual rooms, three physical education rooms, a large gymnasium . . . an administrative suite, and an auditorium that can seat 2,500." The arched concrete roof structure in this photograph enclosed the original cafeteria. As a modern high school, Highland High provided parking for 750 cars, along with a football stadium, baseball diamond, and running track. (Courtesy USHS.)

CLAYTON JUNIOR HIGH SCHOOL, 1959. Clayton Junior High School was completed in 1959 and included a distinct crescent-shaped wing overlooking Emigration Creek in Wasatch Hollow. The classrooms were accessed through a curved hallway, and the two levels stepped down to the creek to provide grand views, while the north-facing clerestory windows provided natural light. Created by Lowell E. Parrish, the design was to take advantage of the contours of the land, though it would be more costly. (Courtesy USHS.)

J.E. COSGRIFF MEMORIAL CATHOLIC SCHOOL, 1957. The Salt Lake Catholic Diocese approved architect Folsom and Hunt's plans for J.E. Cosgriff Memorial Catholic School in 1956 for opening the following fall term. The eight-grade school was staffed by sisters of the Daughters of Charity order who lived in the adjacent rectory at St. Ambrose Parish (also designed by Folsom and Hunt in 1948). The school remains an active Catholic grade school, though it has added kindergarten and is now run by lay administration and faculty. (Courtesy Steven Cornell.)

FRANKLIN SCHOOL, 1959. The original Franklin School was constructed in 1892 but had to be abandoned to make way for the interchange of Interstate 80 and Interstate 15. The second Franklin School, designed by Bruce J. McDermott and built at a cost of $658,921, opened in September 1959 to serve elementary students from the surrounding Poplar Grove neighborhood. The second iteration of the Franklin School was eventually demolished and replaced with the current Franklin Elementary School on the same site. (Courtesy USHS.)

NIBLEY PARK, 1953. The Nibley Park School was approved for construction in June 1952 to ease congestion at the Columbus and Forest School. The elementary school, designed by Fetzer and Fetzer, cost $480,105 to be built by Jensen Construction. It was built alongside two other elementary schools, Glendale Park (designed by Scott and Beecher) and Grandview (designed by Lowell E. Parrish). (Courtesy USHS.)

SALT LAKE CITY BOARD OF EDUCATION, 1966. The First Congregational Church, immediately west of the board of education building, had already been abandoned and sold to the school board by the time it was torched by an arsonist on June 27, 1965. Luckily, the church had already moved its organ and other valuable fixtures and furnishings to its new home on Foothill Drive by the time of the fire. The board of education built a handsome annex on the corner of 400 East and 100 South in 1966. Both the addition and the original board of education building were demolished in 2022 for new offices. (Courtesy USHS.)

SALT LAKE CITY BOARD OF EDUCATION BUILDING, 1938. The Works Progress Administration (WPA) built the new board of education administration building, completed in October 1938, although work was halted a number of times because the school board lacked its $65,000 portion of the $121,000 funding. The site originally housed the Twelfth Ward School, which was eventually razed to make room for the WPA building. Salt Lake City Board of Education offices were housed in the city and county building prior to completion of the new structure. (Courtesy USHS.)

Eight

ARTS, SPORTS, AND RECREATION ARCHITECTURE

RITZ BOWLING ALLEY, 1938. Verne McCullough opened the Ritz "bowling palace" in January 1938 to meet the demand for bowling in Salt Lake City, which had three bowling alleys at the time. Bowling was seen as a fitting offseason activity for "the golfers, the baseball players, tennis players, football players and other sportsters," as described by the *Salt Lake Tribune* in its announcement of the new facility. The Ritz featured a tavern with "Fisher Beer on Draught," a restaurant "equipped with Salt Lake's first complete 'HOT POINT' All-Electric Kitchen," and ample parking. The building was designed by Paulson-Parrish Architect and built by general contractor Roydon K. McCullough at a cost of $150,000. (Courtesy USHS.)

RITZ BOWLING ALLEY, DESIGN. The modernist aesthetic of the Ritz's glimmering facade was reflected in the voluminous interiors of the bowling alley, which contained 18 lanes. At the time, "pin monkeys" sat perched at the end of the lane to place pins into the setting machine and send balls back to bowlers, who manually kept score on stands in the front row. Before mechanical air blowers were used to keep clammy hands dry, the lanes were outfitted with towel holders. The Ritz was located at 925 South Main Street, now the site of an auto body shop. (Courtesy USHS.)

DERKS FIELD, 1940S. The original Derks Field—destroyed by fire in 1946—was built in 1928 by a coalition called the Salt Lake Community Baseball Club that was concerned with keeping baseball in the area following the Pacific Coast League Salt Lake Bees' move to Hollywood. A new Derks Field was built swiftly during the 1946 offseason to appease skeptical Pioneer League executives, although the new grandstand was not quite ready for opening day 1947. (Courtesy USHS.)

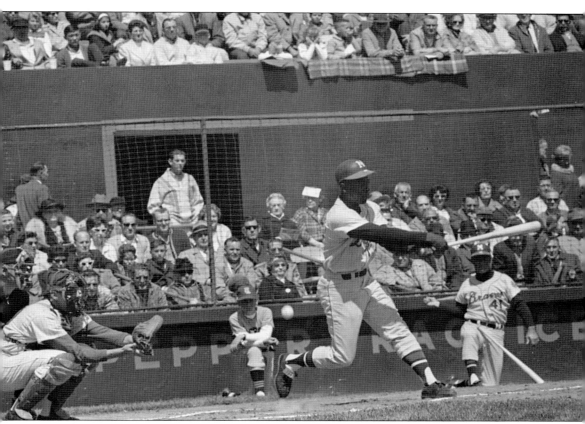

DERKS FIELD, EXHIBITION GAME. The mid-century incarnation of the Salt Lake Bees hosted exhibition games from time to time, including the National League's Milwaukee Braves on April 12, 1964. In this photograph from that game, hall-of-famer Hank Aaron swings and misses at a pitch, while fellow hall of fame member Eddie Mathews (No. 41) looks on from the on deck circle. (Courtesy USHS.)

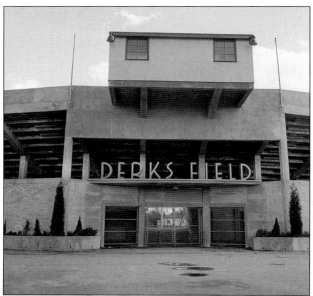

DERKS FIELD, EXPANSION. The Class-C Salt Lake Bees played 11 seasons at the second iteration of Derks Field before Salt Lake once again lured a Pacific Coast League franchise to town. The stadium was expanded from 5,000 to 10,000 seats in 1958 to accommodate the promotion. A variety of teams would call Derks Field home, including the Giants, Angels, Gulls, and Trappers. Derks Field was demolished in 1993 to make way for a new Pacific Coast League franchise, the Salt Lake Buzz. Baseball is still played on the site, with the newest version of the Salt Lake Bees taking the field at Smith's Ballpark, at least for the time being. (Courtesy USHS.)

VILLA THEATRE, 1949. The Villa Theatre, located at 3092 South Highland Drive, opened on December 23, 1949. Designed by A.B. Paulson and built by the Carl S. Fors Company, the movie palace featured over 3,000 yards of velour draperies in the form of a chartreuse main curtain and "coral pink with heavy gold braid tassels" side curtains as well as a modernist mural by San Francisco artist R. Ashby Eccles in the lobby depicting a Utah fishing scene, as reported in the December 22, 1949, *Salt Lake Telegram*. A large, curved marquee with scrolling neon dominated the exterior. The Villa opened with a screening of *Prince of Foxes*, starring Tyrone Power, Orson Welles, and Wanda Hendrix. The theater would eventually house a Cinerama system and remain a movie theater until 2003, when the building became an exotic rug showroom. (Courtesy USHS.)

TOWER THEATER, 1928. When it was first opened in 1928, the Tower Theater featured turreted brick towers flanking a central entrance. By mid-century, however, the theater needed refurbishment and renovations. (Courtesy USHS.)

TOWER THEATER AND TOWER HOUSE, 1950. The Tower Theater shut down for the second half of 1949, showing the film *Tell It to the Judge* in its January 1950 reopening weekend. The new Tower featured a sleek terra-cotta facade, Herculite glass doors, an expanded concession stand, a new marquee, and reupholstered seats and drapes. William J. Monroe Jr. designed the theater renovations, while prolific architect Slack Winburn designed a new storefront for the Tower House, a coffee shop that was opened at the time of the new theater; the combined theater and coffee shop costs were $100,000. The Tower Theater is the longest-running movie theater venue in Utah, and it currently screens art house movies and hosts Sundance Film Festival events (although it has been temporarily shuttered since 2020 for interior remodeling). (Courtesy USHS.)

CLASSIC BOWL, 1958. The invention of mechanical pin setting allowed bowling to become very popular by the 1950s, with alleys opening nationwide, television shows featuring the sport, and outdoor tournaments staged in sports stadiums. Classic Bowl opened in 1958 just as beer league bowling was in its heyday in Utah. (Courtesy USHS.)

CLASSIC BOWL, SIGN. The caption of the March 4, 1959, *Salt Lake Tribune* read, "It was a genuine 'strike' for Tuesday's fierce winds as they toppled the giant bowling pin sign at Classic Bowl, 2255 S. State. The heavy sign crushed four automobiles and a pickup truck owned by adjacent Hinckley Motor Co." Winds of up to 65 miles per hour were reported by the paper. The Classic Bowl sign was fixed and reinstalled, going on to become a mainstay visible from Interstate 80 at the State Street exit. Even after the bowling alley was demolished in 2015, the sign was restored and rebranded to advertise apartments built on the site. (Courtesy USHS.)

LIBERTY PARK CAROUSEL, 1967. The historic wooden carousel at Liberty Park was the victim of an arsonist in the early morning hours of May 22, 1966, with flames visible from the mouth of Big Cottonwood Canyon. Park concessionaire Richard A. Gardiner, who lost about $100,000 worth of property in the fire, vowed immediately to rebuild, and a new $31,756 modernist carousel was opened on April 2, 1967. (Courtesy Steven Cornell.)

WILSON PAVILION AT TRACY AVIARY, 1970. The Tracy Aviary first opened in the southwest corner of Liberty Park during the summer of 1938 when Russel L. Tracy donated 200 birds from his collection along with a $5,000 grant. The pavilion, named after longtime curator Calvin D. Wilson, was built in 1970 at a cost of $128,445 by Herm Hughes Sons Inc. The octagonal form is comprised of sloped glue-laminated wood beams resting on exposed aggregate piers. The Tracy Aviary has expanded since 1970, with the Wilson Pavilion currently housing the South American collection. (Courtesy Steven Cornell.)

ROSE PARK GOLF CLUBHOUSE, 1962. In the summer of 1962, Salt Lake City awarded the contract to construct a new clubhouse at Rose Park Golf Course to Austin L. Hughes, a Bountiful, Utah, contractor, for $108,243. The city added nine additional holes to the existing nine at the same time as the clubhouse construction. Golf had exploded in popularity as people watched the likes of Jack Nicklaus, Arnold Palmer, and Gary Player on television. Rose Park Golf Course was also the home course for current PGA Tour professional Tony Finau as he grew up in the surrounding neighborhood. (Courtesy USHS.)

FAIRMOUNT PARK SWIMMING POOL. Fairmount Park (now Fairmont Park) was a popular Sugar House hangout just north of Forest Dale Golf Course. The Fairmount pool and its Art Deco pump house stood a few hundred feet northeast of the historic Forest Dale Clubhouse but were demolished in the 1960s to make way for Interstate 80. Fairmont Park remains popular for soccer, skateboarding, and picnics, and a modern indoor pool was eventually built in the northeast corner of the park to replace the demolished outdoor one. (Courtesy USHS.)

DESERET GYMNASIUM, 1965. The Deseret Gymnasium moved from its historical 1910 building into its new facility in January 1965, with a ribbon cutting attended by LDS church president David O. McKay. The new building featured all the modern amenities of a mid-century recreation center, including two pools (complete with an underwater intercom), saunas, basketball courts, and a mezzanine running track. Designed by architects Cannon & Mullen, the Deseret Gymnasium was bulldozed in 1997 to make way for the LDS Conference Center. (Courtesy USHS.)

SALT PALACE, 1969. Construction began on the $17-million Salt Palace in 1968, around the time Madison Square Garden opened in New York City. The two structures both used a cable suspension roof system, complete with a massive center "tension ring" (the Salt Palace ring was 100 tons) as a means of providing unobstructed views of the playing surface. The Salt Palace was designed by Bonneville Architects, a partnership Harold K. Beecher and Bruce J. McDermott formed specifically for the project. The original bid was $4 million over budget, leading to a symphony hall being eliminated from the project. (Courtesy USHS.)

THE UTAH STARS. Public reception of the arena was mixed after its 1969 opening, as it operated at a loss before hosting its first professional sports team, the Utah Stars of the American Basketball Association, who moved from Los Angeles to begin play in 1970. The Stars were successful on the court, winning the ABA championship in 1970–1971, but financial struggles led to the team folding in 1975. (Courtesy USHS.)

THE UTAH JAZZ. The Salt Palace was empty for a relatively short time, as Salt Lake City lured the New Orleans Jazz in 1979, and the new Utah Jazz played its first game in the Salt Palace in 1979. The Jazz called the arena home until the Delta Center opened following the 1990–1991 season. The Salt Palace was eventually razed in 1994. (Courtesy UUSC.)

ABRAVANEL HALL, 1979. Previously housed at the Salt Lake Tabernacle on Temple Square, the Utah Symphony found a new home for the latter part of the 1978–1979 season at the Utah Symphony Hall at 123 West South Temple Street. A 1975 bond, along with a contribution from the State of Utah to mark the American Bicentennial of 1976, raised over $10 million for the new Salt Lake County–operated facility. The hall was eventually named after Maurice Abravanel, who was the esteemed musical director and conductor at the time of construction. Considered an acoustical success from its grand opening, the orchestra opened the facility with gala concerts on September 14 and 15, 1979, featuring Stanislaw Skrowaczewski guest conducting Bartok's Concerto for Orchestra and Brahms's Symphony No. 4. The late modernist building was designed by Frank Ferguson, a partner at Fowler & Ferguson. (Courtesy Steven Cornell.)

BIBLIOGRAPHY

Carter, Thomas, and Peter Goss. *Utah's Historic Architecture, 1847–1940*. Salt Lake City: Utah State Historical Society, 1988.

Daily Utah Chronicle (University of Utah). www.newspapers.com.

Deseret News (Salt Lake City). www.newspapers.com .

Deseret Evening News (Salt Lake City). www.newspapers.com.

Salt Lake Evening Chronicle. www.newspapers.com.

Salt Lake Herald. www.newspapers.com.

Salt Lake Herald-Republican. www.newspapers.com.

Salt Lake Telegram. www.newspapers.com.

Salt Lake Tribune. www.newspapers.com.

Sugar House Bulletin (Salt Lake City). www.newspapers.com

Utah Statesman. www.newspapers.com.

INDEX OF ARCHITECTS

ABOUT THE ORGANIZATION

Established in 1966, Preservation Utah (formerly the Utah Heritage Foundation) was the first statewide nonprofit preservation organization in the western United States. Preservation Utah's mission is to keep the past alive, not only for preservation but also to inspire and provoke a more creative present and sustainable future. Preservation Utah preserves, promotes, and protects Utah's historic built environment through public awareness, advocacy, and active preservation.

DISCOVER THOUSANDS OF LOCAL HISTORY BOOKS FEATURING MILLIONS OF VINTAGE IMAGES

Arcadia Publishing, the leading local history publisher in the United States, is committed to making history accessible and meaningful through publishing books that celebrate and preserve the heritage of America's people and places.

Find more books like this at
www.arcadiapublishing.com

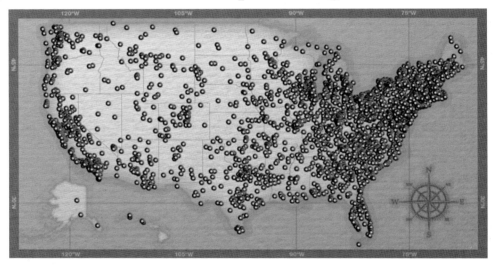

Search for your hometown history, your old stomping grounds, and even your favorite sports team.

Consistent with our mission to preserve history on a local level, this book was printed in South Carolina on American-made paper and manufactured entirely in the United States. Products carrying the accredited Forest Stewardship Council (FSC) label are printed on 100 percent FSC-certified paper.

MADE IN THE USA